The Self Help and Self Esteem Booster for Introvert People

Replace Depression and Anxiety with Positive Thinking and Boost your Confidence in Relationships and Business. (2021 Edition)

Fuller Nadia

Table of Contents

Introduction 1

Chapter 1: What is Self-esteem, what is Self-confidence, What Are the Strengths and Weaknesses of Introverts 3

    Weaknesses of Being an Introvert 6

        You Get Overlooked 6

        You Appear Snobbish 6

        Lack of a Wide Network 6

        Workplace Struggles 6

        Bad First Impression 7

    Strengths of Being an Introvert 7

        Focused 7

        They Think A Lot 7

        Great Listeners 8

        Planners 8

        They Tend to Be Creative 8

        Quiet, So Less problematic - Most of The Time 9

        They Are Less Reckless 10

        Tend to Cultivate Better Relationships 10

Chapter 2: Introvert People and Relationships; Difficulties, Practical Tips to Improve your Relationships (With Friends and Your Partner for Men and Women) 12

    Differing Communications Styles 12

        Being Quiet Can be Read Wrong in A Conflict 13

Conflicting Needs with Your Partner/Friends 14

You Don't Like Talking About Yourself 15

Over-Thinking 16

You Struggle in A Group Setting 16

Ways to Build Better Relationships as an Introvert 18

Embrace Yourself 18

Use Your Knack for Listening to Your Advantage 19

Accept Invitations to Parties Sometimes 19

Be Kind to Strangers 20

Create Small Talk Around Topics You Enjoy 21

Chapter 3: Introvert People and Business: Common Difficulties, Solutions, and Tips on How to Be a Good Leader as an Introvert and How to Succeed in Work or Business as an Introvert 23

Difficulties an Introvert Faces in Work and Business Situations 24

You Will Be Overlooked for Promotions 24

You Do Not Work Well in Teams 25

Lowered Productivity in Open Plan Setting 26

The Stress May Get to You 27

Poor Networks 28

How to Succeed at Work 29

Start Working from the End 29

Take Time to Prepare 29

Schedule Your Breaks 30

Be Knowledgeable in Your Field 30

Their Listening Skills Help Them Understand Better the People They

Lead 31
    They Focus on Their Job 32
    They Are Thorough, Thus Solve Problems Better 32

Chapter 4: How to Destroy Negative Thoughts in Your Life: Tips and Practical Advice 35
Changing Your Self-Perception 35
Improving the Sense of Self Awareness 37
Encouraging Rational Ideas 39
Adopting a New Lifestyle 40
Intentional Exposure 42

Chapter 5: Understand and Control Your Emotions 44
Understand Your Emotions 44
Controlling Your Emotions 46

Chapter 6: Overcoming Lack of Motivation: Strategies and Practical Tips 53
Causes of Lack of Motivation 54
    Falling Below the Threshold 54
    Feeling of Depression 55
    Confusion and Overwhelm 55
    Pleasing Everyone 56
    A Fixed Mindset 57
    Contentment 57
How to Overcome Motivation 58
    Focusing on the Prize 58
    Input Where You Work 59
    Have a Vision of Success? 59
        Fragment Your Tasks 60

Objectify Your Goals 60

Routine Change 61

Chapter 7: How to Think Positive in Your Everyday Life to Reach Your Goals 62

The Wheel of Positive Thinking 63

How to Shift the Wave to Positivity in Order to Achieve Your Goals 65

Do Not Exaggerate 65

Block Negativity 66

Elicit the Positive 66

Embrace It 67

Let Go 67

Motivate 68

Remaining Positive 69

Self-Responsibility 69

Accept Compliments and Critic 70

Chapter 8: Practical Strategies to Overcome Fear ... 71

Facts About Fear 71

Ways of Overcoming Fear 73

Chapter 9: Overcoming Anxiety and Depression 81

Signs of Anxiety and Depression 81

Ways of Creating Positive Affirmations 83

Advantages of Positive Thinking 86

How to Be Positive Minded 87

Chapter 10: Mental Toughness 92

Overcome Resistance That Keeps You from Moving Forward 92

What Are the Factors That Cause Mental Toughness? 95

Structural Resistances 102
Personal Resistance 103

Introduction

Thank you for choosing this book, dear reader. Through the countless options that were available, that you chose this book means that you felt we had what you needed. And guess what? We got you!

So, you look at yourself and come to the realization that, unlike many people around, you, you are not very outgoing, unless it is under specific circumstances, you enjoy your alone time more than when you are in company and you tend to be so lost in your thoughts that you practically live there and only come into the real universe for some juice and snacks. You look in the mirror and all that you've read about personalities come back to you in droves. Gasp! You are an introvert! And as you are wont to do, you begin to draw graphs and pages of dissertation about what this means. Are you unfriendly? Arrogant? Do you hate people?

The thing is, being introverted is a personality trait that will often result in you being ignored since you tend to 'disappear' when around people. And being an introvert is not made any better when you look around the world and realize that it is built to accommodate more extroverted people than people like you, with more introverted tendencies. The workplace, schools, and even at home, they are all designed to make us go out and meet people, regardless of whether you want to or not.

In this book, we are going to cover ways in which you can come to terms with your introversion and succeed in a world built for the extroverts. And you won't need to shed your introversion. Instead, we will teach you how to harness it and build relationships, both at home and in the workplace, how you can overcome the fear of getting started and just doing it.

Chapter 1: What is Self-esteem, what is Self-confidence, What Are the Strengths and Weaknesses of Introverts

In the world that we live in, it is easy to get lost in the hustle and bustle of the fast-paced happenings around us. So much so that, one finds themselves unable to take time and sit down and reflect on how they are going through life. Am I living indeed? Or am I just drifting like a paper boat in the river? What drives me? And what gives me my self-confidence? What kind of person am I, and how do I interact with the world outside?

Well, in all honesty, sitting down and reflecting can be, well, tiresome for some, and uncomfortable and exhausting for others, especially with so many exciting things going on around us. The little screen beckons on your palm. On the other end, your job calls, to your other side, the family wants a piece of you. Ahead of you, your friends want to know what your plans for Friday are. Then, they want to know your plans for Monday and Tuesday and the rest of the year. Behind you, well, many other things going on but we are not in a horror movie so we won't focus on what's behind you. That's for you to figure it out. Sorry.

So, now that I have your attention, what exactly do we consider our self-esteem? What comes to mind when we talk of self-esteem? Is it your job that gives you so much joy? Your family and friends? Your downtime?

Well, we have come to think of self-esteem and self-confidence as two of the same, and we use them interchangeably most of the time. But down to the finer details, these two are different. You could, for example, be someone who has very high self-esteem but then, suffer frequently from bouts of low self-confidence. Yes, you look at this text funny, but it's possible and accurate.

Self-esteem refers to how you view yourself generally. This view is often shaped by what we have experienced and how we then were able to react to our experiences. People who have gone through trauma or abuse, for example, may have low self-esteem. This issue is because the experiences subjected them to negative experiences that stressed them to the point that they lost hope in their existence. Your self-esteem means being comfortable in your entire humanity, down to those bits of yourself that perhaps are embarrassing or shameful. It is about knowing how you feel, act, think, behave, and how that shapes your existence in the world today.

Self-confidence, on the other hand, is your ability to trust in yourself and rise to new challenges. Often, one builds their confidence through their achievements and skills. Unlike self-esteem, which touches based on one's entire person (the physical, emotional, mental, and spiritual) and therefore once built can be hard to shake, self-confidence may vary from one situation to another. Since it we link it to abilities and one that people tie to high visibility, it can, therefore, change with regards to the situation. So, for example, I may be a person with very high self-esteem, but I am not good at solving complex mathematical problems, then I will experience low self-confidence in situations that would need me to focus on mathematical problems.

The above passage then brings us then to introverts and how self-esteem and self-confidence will come out different in a brooder.

Many people conflate introversion with shyness, which may not be necessarily true. Shyness is a state of being that we link to social anxiety and the inability of a shy person to create contact with other people. One can be shy either from nature or nurture. On most occasions, self-esteem and self-confidence could be low in a shy person. Shyness always means that the shy person is willing to go out and make friends, but their low view of themselves (low self-esteem) and their abilities (self-confidence) hold them back.

However, an introvert is someone who often loves to spend time on their own because that is where they get their energy. The introverts are happier, more at ease when they are alone. While introversion and shyness may overlap, they do not always occur at the same time all the time. An introvert maybe someone who is adept at making friends, and they may be socially well-adjusted and confident, with high self-esteem, but because their brain is wired in such a way that they function better and are happier and more productive when in their own company, they often tend to spend a significant chunk of their time alone, preferably indoors. An introvert will usually avoid the spotlight.

So, since the introverts love spending time on their own, surely there are downsides to that. Yes, indeed, there are weaknesses in being introverted.

Weaknesses of Being an Introvert
You Get Overlooked
As we said early in the chapter, as an introvert, you tend to get lost in your world, even when with others. So, this can lead to you being overlooked and ignored in a group setting.

You Appear Snobbish
Because of an introvert's desire to avoid being the center of attention, you will then avoid making overtures to other people. You will avoid making small talks for fear of the awkwardness that comes with it, and you will turn down invitations to parties and events. These situations then mean that people will label you as a snob to may who do not understand you. Thus, people will avoid you because of this.

Lack of a Wide Network
To grow in many things, one needs a network, and to build a network, you will need to go out there and meet people. But this is not easy for an introvert. They want their space for themselves and may find networking stressful and thus avoid it entirely doesn't mean that they are incapable of networking. They do not want the stress that comes from being around many people at once, trying to build rapport. An introvert will want to be social at their convenience, which, unfortunately, is not how the world works.

Workplace Struggles
Because of their dislike of shallow socialization, many introverts will often struggle with workplace interactions, which calls for frequent interactions between colleagues but does not allow for the formation of deep, meaningful bonds

between co-workers. As such, because of their distaste for pointless interactions, they will often avoid the situations that need them to be or do that, thus, will not create the impression that they value teamwork, even when the reality is quite different. As we said earlier, the workplace and school are built for extroverts, so, the introverts will often not get their end of the bargain met.

Bad First Impression

Let's be honest p- we often make judgments about other people based on our first interaction with them. As such, the first impression matters a lot and often goes a long way to shape how you interact further with the new stranger.

For an introvert, though, their dislike for the spot often means that they will appear aloof when meeting new people. Because they are so protective of their personal space, they will appear unfriendly and rude. This situation could be damaging to an introvert's limited but highly valuable social life.

But there are strengths to this too.

Strengths of Being an Introvert

Focused

Because of their desire to avoid too much clutter, introverts will often tend to be more focused and may become more productive at work or in school.

They Think A Lot

The word introvert comes from introspecting. An introvert, therefore, will more likely be a person who is often deeply engaged in their thought process. Because they spend a lot of time on their own, they develop an inner voice that allows them to build their self-awareness, which makes them likely to become better problem solvers.

Many critical thinkers have been described as introverts, among them Albert Einstein, Charles Darwin, and Sir Isaac Newton. Albert Einstein has often been quoted saying that the monotony that came with being on your own is what stimulates creativity, which then would explain why many of the most prominent thinkers are introverts.

Great Listeners

Introverts tend to be great listeners. Because they think a lot to themselves, they become more aware of how their actions affect the world around them. This ability then makes them more willing to listen to others and thus, make great friends.

The fact that they talk less also makes them unlikely to interfere when the other person tells.

Planners

An introvert will often do the most to avoid being in the spotlight, whether for wrong reasons or the right reasons. If their boss calls them to, say, make a presentation, an introvert will take their time to make the preparations necessary to carry through the situation. This ability to make a point of making sufficient preparation means that they will often avoid being caught flat-footed and they will ensure that they say the right things when the time comes. This preparation allows them to become great orators.

They Tend to Be Creative

While this is not true for all creatives and all introverts, being introverts makes it more likely that one can develop their creativity. In solitude, an introvert may find that they spend more time in their thoughts, which allows for ideas to form and evolve. Among the many introverted creatives are; the father of modern horror H. P Lovecraft, Harry Porter Creator J.K Rowling, Dr. Seuss among others.

Creativity tends to need time for creative person to be on their own so that it can develop. In a rush to do one thing or another, the creative mind, which is spontaneous, will be stifled under the stress of plans and schedules and will often be buried deep when one is continuously in motions. Therefore, the ability for the creative to find peace and calm, even when they are in the presence of noise and distraction is a testament to how may introvert can dominate the creative field. Plus, because many creative projects often mean working alone most of the time, at least, this is heaven to the introvert who prefers solitude. And if you are an introvert and can make a career out of your solitude fortress, then why not?

Quiet, So Less problematic - Most of The Time

Now this is not to say that extroverts are problematic, though to be honest, aren't they?

However, as we have said, introverts do not thrive when under too much attention, or when put under the spotlight. This revelation means that their being quiet is often a way of drawing attention away from themselves, which makes them then a darling in situations that requires repose and calmness.

Unlike the extrovert who is more outgoing and gets energized when around others, an introvert will often want to maintain their peace and will thus, be unlikely to cause problems. They will not court unnecessary controversy or perform things they do not feel comfortable doing. This situation then means that having them around, say as friends and family at a time when you want someone to be around to keep you company is glorious.

They Are Less Reckless

This advantage is because introverts are naturally inclined to be deliberative and thoughtful. Because an introvert spends more time observing, thinking, and reflecting, they often gain a deeper understanding of whatever they want to do. This understanding then allows them to gauge what the risks and paybacks for a particular course of action are worth it. This ties in later to their need to plan to the last detail.

As such, they may then make better leaders since they will often try to find the best course of action which they wouldn't want to regret later. As such, they avoid making hasty choices

Tend to Cultivate Better Relationships

This point is again, not to say that extroverts don't form great relationships. However, some of the predisposing traits of introversion make them more likely to want to create a strong personal bond, over them becoming popular among a large group of people.

Again, we can tie this to many of their other traits. Because of their tendency to think a lot, and more deeply, they will extend their trust to very few people, with the intent of forming deep, meaningful relationships with them. As a result, because of their ability to listen better and take their time to think through things, they often gain the complete trust of the people that they allow into their world, which allows for more vulnerable, cherished interactions with their friends.

Chapter 2: Introvert People and Relationships; Difficulties, Practical Tips to Improve your Relationships (With Friends and Your Partner for Men and Women)

As we have seen in chapter one, while introverts do not have what we can describe as a bustling social life, they still do value the relationships that they form and thus, will often want to maintain them.

This situation then means that the introvert may be compelled to move out of their comfort zones so that they maintain the relationships that they have formed and that they value.

The thing with introverts is that, for the most part, they will often form relationships that they want to establish. The people that they keep around, the people that they hang around are usually people that the introvert wants to have around.

Now, as with any relationship out there, you will come across relationship problems as an introvert. In your case, though, your introversion makes things a little more complicated. For example;

Differing Communications Styles

How many times have you and the people in your life fought? If we are honest, it is a couple of times, if it's a healthy relationship.

Now, when you look at things from your perspective, you often take the time just after a bit of confrontation to get lost in your thoughts momentarily. Because of this, the person in your life may come to take this as a sign that you are avoiding them when in reality, you are accepting the time, as you are wont to do, to comb through your thoughts.

Extroverts often find that they are more responsive in a fast-paced scenario. If you are an introvert and you begin dating an extrovert, the different ways that you communicate could create some friction between the two of you.

Communication is an integral part of a healthy relationship. Therefore, as an introvert, your desire to be in your own world and make worlds out of your own thoughts will often mean that you will place little value and emphasis on the real-world relationships that you have, leading to a nasty breakdown in communication, which is only the first step in a decreasing value of the connection.

As stated, a few introverts may also suffer from shyness, which would then mean that they will have an even harder time communicating effectively due to their low confidence and social anxiety. This situation can crumble the relationship.

Being Quiet Can be Read Wrong in A Conflict

How many events of conflict have you found yourself in? Probably more than a few times, right?

The thing is that, because of their quiet and calm demeanor, introverts will often not display their full range of emotions. When they are angry, they will often talk will composure, and when things indeed do get to a head, rather than explode (unless really pushed), an introvert will sit back quietly and ruminate. You have done it, right?

Now, many people out here are extroverts. They understand that conflict is an exchange that has both people going at each other. However, in your case, your silence and calmness can be looked at as a lack of concern or as a show that you do not value what the other person is saying. If you are at work and it is your boss confronting you, you may inexplicably be giving off the vibe that you do not take what they are saying seriously.

If you disagree with your significant other, you may come off as being arrogant towards them, as uncaring, even when this is not true. When you do not take care, this situation can lead to a breakdown in communication, which could adversely affect your relationships, which means so much to you.

Conflicting Needs with Your Partner/Friends

When you date someone o is more outgoing, the chances are that your personalities may overlap and cross paths.

So, there you are, having gotten used to spending your quality time alone, curled up on a sofa with a book perhaps, or a movie. Then you get into a relationship and suddenly, you need to make plans to go out with your partner.

While these kinds of differences can be ironed out with communication, there is still often that feeling of dissatisfaction when you push yourself to get out more and become more outgoing, which can result in frequent problems between you and your spouse.

When you and your partner go out, and they need to take a picture, you will have to do it, even when you are uncomfortable with it. These kinds of situations always arise and may lead to conflicts.

You Don't Like Talking About Yourself.

Imagine yourself going out on a first date. Wow! Butterflies and all! But then you get there, and immediately you realize that you may not be too keen to talk about yourself to this new person. Even after a few dates, you may still not be comfortable.

This desire to not reveal too much about themselves will often cost many introverts relationships.

To build relationships requires that we become comfortable in being vulnerable with the other person. This helps foster trust and allows people to bond more deeply.

While an introvert will cherish the chance to form deep bonds with others, the thing is that they will often do that in the hopes that they do not get to reveal too much about themselves. It is usually not because they have something to hide. Perhaps it is because they may feel overwhelmed then or probably may not be too deep in the relationship yet. Introverts take their time to build relationships, which then, can make a frustrating experience for the extroverted friend or partner.

Because of your lack of desire to talk about yourself, you may then come off as disinterested, and perhaps the partner may interpret this as a sign that you do not value them.

Over-Thinking

Hey, thinking is great! You sure do know that. But then, as with anything else, it can become problematic when overdone.

The natural tendency of an introvert to become obsessed with details and planning and observing and decoding will often mean that they approach almost everything from a thinker's perspective.

In shopping, you obsess over the choices you are to make. The jam is too sugary, but the marmalade that you want has run out. The alternative jelly looks good, but it is from a brand you don't know, but the third option looks promising. The fourth option appears like a cheap knock-off of your fave. The fifth option is far down, and so on.

This issue can be frustrating to the people that are in your life. Because of your desire to make the right decision, your obsession with details might create a wedge between you and the people around you.

In this case, this scenario could lead to your friends and partners avoiding you as you begin to become dull.

While it may appear superficial and vain, overthinking may be counterproductive in the long-term as this will mean that you get caught in the paradox of choice, and you may end up choosing the worse option.

You Struggle in A Group Setting

As we have stated, as an introvert, you find great solace in your own company. In that alone time, that is often most of the time, you brainstorm ideas, create stories and drawn art.

You toy around with thoughts and ideas and concepts. Essentially, you become your biggest library.

But then, when you go out with your friends, you find yourself as part of a group. Suddenly, doors close shut in your mind. The stories you wanted to tell are locked inside. With all the people around, the interactions drain all your energy. Unable to access your inner thoughts, you become quiet in the group, and you come off as just a hanger-on. Your friends begin to think that you do not value the relationship, even when you reassure them that you do. Your actions seem not to match your words.

Being an introvert means that it is hard to survive in situations that acknowledges extroversion.

What this does then is, it can create friction between you and your friends. You will appear stuck-up and unwilling to take part in the interactions, even though the truth is that you are not really able to access your best thoughts in a group setting. This is also frustrating to you as an introvert too. You can't adequately explain why you do not know how to think well when with others. As such, it becomes hard to create a connection with others.

If it is in your romantic relationship when your partner begins to take note that you enjoy being on your own, perhaps more than you enjoy being with them, they will distance themselves too, in the knowledge that you do not need them.

So, to avoid these scenarios, what could be the solutions?

Ways to Build Better Relationships as an Introvert

Embrace Yourself

Because of the cynical view that people attach to the introvert, it might be easy then for some introverts to go to extreme lengths to create a fake extroverted exterior so that they can obtain other people's approval.

The obvious thing here is that you are already setting up the relationship for failure by pretending to be someone you are not, which is dishonesty. Aside from this, though, you will be unable to communicate well how you feel about things and thus, will be forced to double down so that you do not sell yourself out. This occurrence goes on and on until it gets to a point where you can't take it any longer, and you snap. Things change suddenly, and now, your relationships stand on the brink of collapse, balancing precariously on the edge of a precipice

You can avoid this. To build better relationships, many relationship experts will advise that you first begin by loving yourself. As an introvert, this will mean coming to terms with your introversion and understanding how you communicate and how you want others to communicate with you. What is your love language? How do you show your displeasure? What words of affirmation do you use, and which ones do you appreciate when someone tells you? How do you like to be touched? What gestures do you want? Gifts? Words?

Only through becoming comfortable with yourself will you then be able to move on to the other steps.

Use Your Knack for Listening to Your Advantage

This skill is one of your key strengths as an introvert. As such, it can be a powerful tool to use to create a better rapport with the people that you come into contact with or interact with.

But now, to build from this, rather than just listening, take time after the other person is done talking to say back what they have said to you. This active strategy will allow you to gauge how well you listen while also letting the other person know that someone is listening to them. People often will feel closer to other people that make them feel worthy. By repeating back what the other person has said (not in the exact words obviously) you tell them indirectly that you value them and want to interact more with them. You will find that you will create better relationships without having to pretend to be outgoing or loud.

Also, listen to learn about the other person. You will be amazed at how this will quickly allow you to bond with them.

Accept Invitations to Parties Sometimes

Yes, I know this freaks you out, but social circles are often built and maintained by frequent time spent together. When you have friends, and they make the point to include you to events, you could work with them in how you will accept the invitations.

To create strong bonds with them, being honest with them will create a situation where they can extend an invitation to you, and you can accept some and reject others, or maybe even accept all of them but them come to an agreement with them that you leave early.

We all thrive on social bonds, so don't isolate yourself too much. Say yes to going out sometimes, but of course, not at the expense of your mental state. Your friends should be able to respect the boundaries that you agree on, and you do the same.

Be Kind to Strangers

Well, mainly we should be kind to everyone. But, for the most part, many people are often rude to strangers when it is undeserved. Because of this, it is in many of us a habit to treat strangers with indifference and disdain in some instances.

As an introvert trying to build better relationships, try by being the opposite - be kind to strangers. What this does is that it helps you acknowledge the humanity of the other person. by being thankful to the cashier, you begin to tell them that they matter. By pardoning the person that stepped on your toes, you tell them that you acknowledge that to err is human.

When you are with your friends, this will help them feel more connected to you and want to associate with you. You will win their admiration, and they will most likely want to associate more with you.

On the other hand, you will create a vast pool of potential friends with the people that you are kind towards and will have something going. Since you will be making this gesture from your own volition, and not under the pressure of making friends, you will enjoy it, and it will allow you to gain a better perspective of what people want and what they need. Even when your actions do not have the desired effect, you still know that you did your best.

Create Small Talk Around Topics You Enjoy

Small talks are a bore. That much we have established. Often used as a filler for awkward silences, it is often more awkward and bland and often superficial and without direction. For an introvert, who chooses their words carefully, and takes time to think, these kinds of thoughts, of course, makes them want to tear their hair out.

However, while it is indeed true that small talks are mostly terrible, most of it is usually not because of the very concept of small talk, but because very many people out here, both introverts and extroverts, are very terrible communicators. As such, you will find that you are not exactly opposed to small talks as you are to the fact that it will be forced and unnatural.

Therefore, take the time to think of how you would like someone to make small talk with you and where and how. If you are in a position to approach, do it. This approach could be easy to achieve if you attend a function on something you enjoy or consider meaningful.

To do this, take your time. Do not rush into it just because you want to get through it. Give yourself room to grow more comfortable with the idea of going out to strike a conversation.

This point is not to say that you will become someone who will go out and talk to others, but you will know when and how you approach this, thus, still ensuring that you are comfortable with the interaction.

Chapter 3: Introvert People and Business: Common Difficulties, Solutions, and Tips on How to Be a Good Leader as an Introvert and How to Succeed in Work or Business as an Introvert

In business and work situations, building networks is what always leads to one's success. This type of situation often demands that one is capable of fast, easy-going interactions, as you would want to meet and create contact with as many people as possible. This interaction is, of course, the kind of situation that an introvert isn't exactly comfortable with and you will freak out.

As a result, you will find that most introverts have a small network of business and work contacts. While this doesn't necessarily mean that they will not be successful, there is no doubt that in business and work situations, the more you interact with others, the better you build your chances to succeed.

As such, there will be common difficulties that an introvert will encounter in these kinds of situations.

Difficulties an Introvert Faces in Work and Business Situations

You Will Be Overlooked for Promotions

A philosopher once said that 'in the world we live in, confidence is looked at as competence'.

Think of how you go about your business at work. Do you call attention to what you have done? Do you talk up your achievements, or do you avoid them?

You are an introvert, so of course, you will not call attention to what you have done. Studies have revealed that in many organizations, the people that ascend to the higher offices will often be those who display themselves to the world outside like fish drying in the sun. As we evolved, our brains evolved in a way that allowed it to make quick judgments and thus, to efficiently get as much information about the other person as it could with the little knowledge it had in hand. As such, we grew to make conclusions about people based on a few traits, allowing us to move on to other things.

It is for this reason why first impressions are essential, biased, and faulty as they are.

So, using the above as a guide, let us move to your workplace, where we assume that there is a promotion looming. There is your more confident coworker Mary, who will speak up their abilities, even when they are average at best. This talk is a desperate attempt to win the bosses over. It's so apparent that it makes you cringe. You, on the other hand, bury your head in the task and get things done well. Your independence and self-drive allow you to do it with little supervision, meaning that you perhaps don't make an impression with the higher-ups.

But because you dislike attention, you work in silence and do not care anyway. You let your job speak for itself.

Meanwhile, across the office, Mary continues to talk up her abilities. While you wish her all the best, you do know, in your head, that she is not the best fit for the job and the bosses will overlook her. Meanwhile, you work twice as hard and let your job talk even more for you.

Then come, promotion day and - who's that? Mary? You gasp in disbelief! How?

Well, because she made the job easier for the bosses. Because of the bias in our evolution, despite Mary's role being bang average, the fact that she showed a lot of confidence in herself means that the bosses to the conclusion that she was competent and would make a good leader. Despite this assumption being flawed, it is prevalent. We look at the most talkative people as more in control, thus more confident, and thus again, more competent.

As such, your inclination as an introvert to work covertly works against you such a scenario.

You Do Not Work Well in Teams

Most workplaces tend to try to build better relationships between their colleagues by dedicating some tasks to groups or may organize trips and dates out.

These kinds of situations will drain energy off an introvert. What the bosses then nobly believe brings colleagues together only serves to make the introvert more awkward. The fact that working in groups entails a lot of talk and noises and movement is what eats into the introvert's energy.

So, rather than become active, as other members of the team, an introvert will instead find themselves unable to make themselves useful if they are to carry out a task in the group. Their contribution drops because they cannot think straight, as they think better on their own, curled up in a corner, or silently mulling at their desks in serenity.

This act may make you appear antisocial and misanthropic. Of course, there may be introverts out there who do hate people, but we are not talking about them; we are talking about you, a reasonably well-adjusted person who finds your energy in your time alone. So, because of this flaw, you will then be at crossroads with your senior, who may take this as a sign that you do not receive your job seriously, or that you are not willing to push yourself at your job.

Lowered Productivity in Open Plan Setting

An introverts' personal space is one of the things that they value. So, to make them work in a place where they are around a large group of people then means that an introvert is terrified about the situation that feeds off their energy.

Many people, including the extroverts, dislike crowded office spaces. And if an extrovert can be opposed to such a layout, imagine the torture you go through as an introvert? It can be suffocating.

There you are, exposed to other people's spaces. There is noise flying over your head - loud laughter, voices all around, all of which may cause you to develop a mild headache. But then the worse of all is that it then makes it easier for other people to approach you. Yikes! Small talk again.

This reaction doesn't mean that you hate interacting with your coworkers. Instead, you are very selective with whom you chose to interact with, or who you allow into your personal space. Unfortunately, at the workplace, you do not have the luxury to make this selection and will, therefore, need to interact with a lot more people than you may not like. The stress that arises can reduce your productivity.

The Stress May Get to You

When you are forced to act in a manner that is contrary to how you naturally behave, you may experience stress because your body has used up all of the energy. As a result, to cope, you may begin to become more withdrawn.

In many job situations, you will often be required to act as outgoing and extroverted, as this is what the workplace rewards. When you do this repeatedly, and for a long time, and against your will, you will drain yourself of all your energy. Once this happens, you then exhibit stress symptoms.

This situation will often result in you then cutting relations with your coworkers as you feel overwhelmed by the whole idea of interacting with them. Rather than just avoiding interactions with them because that's how you prefer it when you become stressed, you begin to avoid interacting with them because you hate it. The stress has left you worse off, and you now start to despise interactions with your coworkers.

This stress can then result in you acting contrary to how you usually would. In situations where you are calm and collected, you become irritable. When you are stressed, you then begin to show this by not meeting your target. Your productivity drops and your job suffers.

Poor Networks

One of the ways that the business world works hard on the extrovert is that it tends to put more focus on how one presents themselves to the other person. In the business world, first impressions matter a lot. Most people, in networking events, are in a rush to meet as many people as possible. Thus, it becomes hard, then, for you as an introverted entrepreneur to make the right impression properly.

Because you want to take your time to interact, you lose out for the most part since the networking world is fast-paced.

And the thing about networking is, when you get an opportunity, you will need to take it as you do not know when you will get such at any other time. So, there you are, an introvert, brimming with ideas and an impressive resume, but you then feel disabled because you do not know where to begin. The entire situation - the movements, the noise, the small talk that is supposed to create rapport, all works to drain you of your energy. At the end of it all, you find that you have barely made contact.

It can be defeating. And the thing is that no one will approach you when you stand awkwardly at the corner, overwhelmed and over-thinking.

So, is there any solution to this? Yes, and one of the critical strengths of introverts is that they make great leaders. You can use this knowledge of the area to your advantage and use it to build relationships. Many renowned leaders are introverts; Barrack Obama, Mahatma Gandhi, among others.

How to Succeed at Work

Start Working from the End

The worst part about any interaction is that you will need to keep up an act so as you can make it through. With networking, this can mean becoming very uncomfortable as your attempts to build relationships. But stop there.

The thing about the human mind is that, when you visualize how you would wish the end to be, you become more likely to follow through the required actions, even when they may make you uncomfortable. Scientists explain this phenomenon in the reward-motivation theory. When you make a clear vision of the reward, it will act as a motivation that will then see you follow through the required actions.

So, when you go out to network, take time to, not just think but create a clear vision of what you would want to have gained at the end of the interactions.

What this will do is that it will take your mind off the entire process and allow you to look at the interactions more favorably. It will become more comfortable for you to make then the moves that you need to, since, you will not be overthinking about the process but rather, how the end will be of benefit to you.

Take Time to Prepare

When at work, you will need to be comfortable to be in uncomfortable situations. This saying is, unfortunately, the truth. While there are concerted efforts to making the workplace more inclusive to introverts, chances are, there are still many places that haven't picked up on that. This reality means that you will need then to adopt from your end.

To avoid feeling put on the spot, take your time to prepare well, in case it is a meeting, for example. Planning makes you more anticipatory and will make you more comfortable when someone calls for your opinion or input on something. Use your thoughtfulness and time alone to lay down the groundwork for your job interactions. This planning and thoughtfulness will make you less likely to feel put on the spot when you are asked to make a presentation.

Of course, it sometimes happens that what you prepare for may disappear once someone calls you out, as it drains up your energy very fast, but you can never go wrong with a little plan.

Schedule Your Breaks

At the workplace, you will notably be working under the organization's schedule. But you feel like you need to take some time off. When, to avoid putting yourself under a lot of stress, make a point of scheduling short breaks during moments when you feel like you cannot take it. These breaks should allow you to recharge a little, giving you a small break from the office. This way, you bring down your stress levels. These breaks will enable you to also work on your productivity as you are more productive when you are alone and in your zone.

When you make these breaks, be sure to let the colleagues that you are close to knowing about them, so that they will explain this to the outer nucleus of your workplace interactions.

Be Knowledgeable in Your Field

Earlier in chapter one, we talked about how self-confidence varies depending on the situation. Perhaps as an introvert, you may find that you do not interact well with your colleagues and are stressed at the workplace because you do not have confidence in your field.

Well, you could work around this by becoming more knowledgeable in your department. Use your time alone to learn about things that many people may miss on the surface. Go beyond the obvious and dig deeper. Because of your knack for reflecting and breaking things down, you will be able to build the sense of a master around yourself. This ability to take the time and think will then allow you to avoid pointless small talk, and instead, you will be making interactions based on what you know and understand about your field. This knowledge will earn you the respect of your colleagues. However, it is crucial not to overdo it as it will result in the opposite effect. When you become a smart-ass, you push people away. Be wise with your knowledge.

In a different scenario, leadership positions can be useful for an introvert. I know it sounds counter-intuitive since an introvert doesn't like the spot and becoming a leader means being on the place consistently. But leadership roles can be a perfect fit for an introvert for several reasons.

Their Listening Skills Help Them Understand Better the People They Lead

A lot of times, people in leadership positions can be frustrating. Because of the belief that they know more, they tend not to listen to ordinary people. An introvert naturally is someone who will sit quietly and observe and thus will make more accurate assessments of the situation. They will then be able to listen better and work with others to create solutions.

However, this is not just something natural. You will need to horn it through repeated drills, like going through what someone says after they have said it.

Also, you will need to become more visible, which means that you will need to make yourself comfortable with calling meetings and engaging more with others. This break from your usual character will increase your influence and visibility; all of which are necessary components for leadership.

They Focus on Their Job

Introverts will generally be more focused because of their ability to turn out noises. Since they have drawn their energy from within, they are more likely to keep going with something as long as their internal motivation is alive, even when the outside environment changes drastically.'

When in leadership positions, this means that they will be able to keep the motivation of their teams without being distracted by other demands. Also, because of their self-drive, they can build better examples for the people that they lead. They will be able to motivate their teams from just their work alone, without words and many motivational speeches.

They Are Thorough, Thus Solve Problems Better

Being a problem solver is one of the critical ingredients of being a good leader. Introverts are naturally inclined to sit and deliberate before making any decisions.

Researcher Rehana Khalil, in her research paper *'Influence of Extroversion and Introversion in Decision Making Ability,* concluded that introverts made their choice based on their inner feelings and intuitions. Because of this, they will often try to come up with concrete solutions to problems, and will unlikely make snap decisions to get the issue over and done.

Because of their need to take time to mull over a problem, an introvert will be able to come up with better, innovative ways to solving problems. They will be creative and will thus, also allow the team they are leading to be creative, which then means that productivity increases.

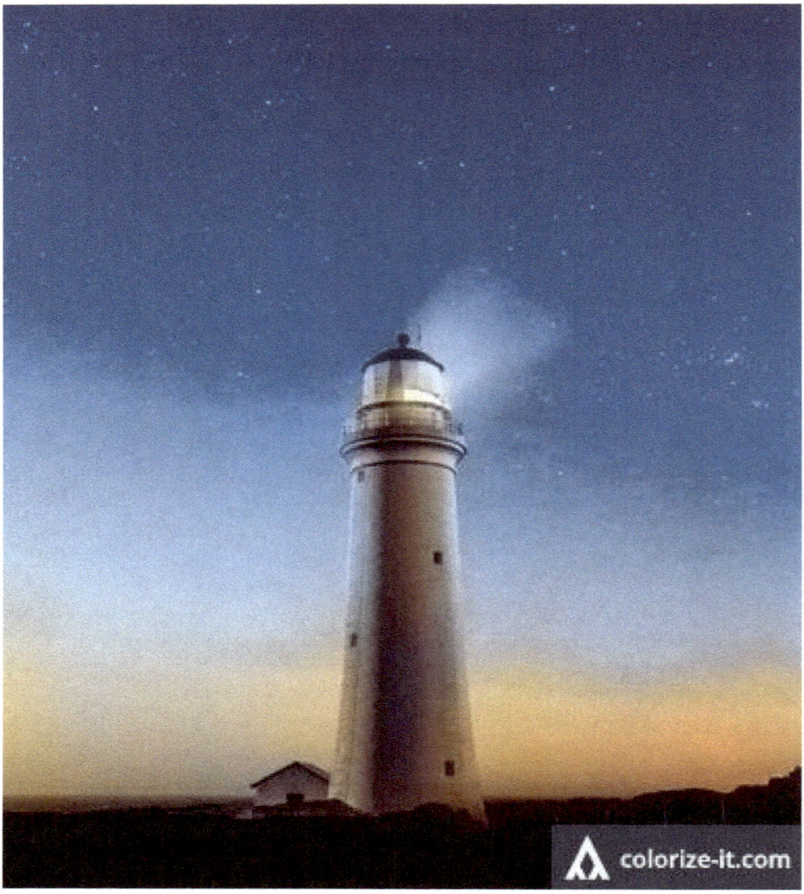
colorize-it.com

Chapter 4: How to Destroy Negative Thoughts in Your Life: Tips and Practical Advice

Changing Your Self-Perception

Thoughts about yourself in terms of who you think you are, what you have done, what you intend to do, what we hope and what we feel about yourself makes you. It is not something that is done within one day, but it is an accumulation of self-impression that happens for a long period. Thoughts that evaluate yourself and others have a very big impact on the way you accept other people, your control in different situations, and self-acceptance. For instance, if you feel that you are not smart enough for your peers, it will affect your interaction and the way you present yourself in the presence of your peers. In this case, you are likely to keep your comments, opinion, and ideas to yourself because you think that they are not good enough. Conversely, if you think that your pears are not good enough, you will also keep your ideas, and comments and opinions to yourself during your interaction with them because you think they might not understand you. This aspect hinders a healthy interaction, making you keep off from the others. It also hinders growth as you may not have an opportunity to experience what the other people are experiencing and try out new things and ideas.

You should remember that you are the one who defines yourself, even if people express their thoughts about you; it is you who will accept them and make them true. If you think that you are a bad person and continue with the same thoughts for a long time, it will surely be true, and the same thing will happen if you think you are good. Therefore, it is good to have positive thoughts about yourself to bring out the positive side of you. It is not bad to have an internal self-critic because it helps you to stay on track and improve yourself, but during your reflection about yourself, you should concentrate on the positive side that makes you a better person. For example, during a football training session, you exchanged insults with your friend for taking his bottle of water. when you go back at home you reflect on what happened and find that although your friend was on the wrong you did not act appropriately by lashing out insults on him, instead you should have asked why he has taken your bottle and listen to his reason. This type of thinking helps you correct the way you react in situations in case you are offended. However, another thought about the incident could be that your friend thought that you are not strong enough to defend yourself, that is why he took your water, and next time, you will give him what he deserves if anyone does the same thing. This is a critic that negative, and it does not improve your self-perception and interaction with other people. Therefore, concentrate on the thoughts that bring out the good in you and lift your spirits, and when criticizing your actions and feelings towards other people always entertain thoughts that improve the situation, and not worsen. Besides, do not let other people's thoughts about you define you; it is only what you think about yourself. Accepting things that cannot be changed about you is also critical because when you accept them in your thoughts, you change your attitude about them and just love yourself the way you are.

Improving the Sense of Self Awareness

It is good to always have good thoughts about yourself; however, they should come with great awareness. This means that you should not get drunk with your goodness, as it can spoil things for you and affect your interaction with the other people. This involves thinking about how you behave in certain situations and why you behave that way. For instance, when in public I worry about what people think about me, and always present myself in a way that will make me appear to be good. I would only eat what my friends eat to appear good in their presence. You appear good in front of your friends, but when you think about it more privately and deeply, it is your goodness in the presence of your friends of any help to you. Remember that there is always a real-life aware of the deceptions, and when it hits you that you have to be real, it becomes difficult to cope. A man who presents himself as wealthy wins the heart of a beautiful girl, and he gives her more expensive gifts to give the impression that he is rich, but in real life, the man is struggling with finances. Things get ugly for him when he marries the lady and reality hits him that he cannot give the lady the expensive life that he had shown him. Coping with the situation becomes difficult and the lady eventually leaves him. The man becomes frustrated but still cannot share with his friend because of fear of embarrassment, and therefore, he keeps everything to himself and pretends to be fine. This man should sit down and have a thought about himself and how he presents himself in the presence of other people, and how it affects him. If presenting good things that you do not have affecting your growth as a person and healthy interactions then it is not good. Self-awareness will help you see, the other side of you that you always hide to appear or to show that you are good. It helps you to work on our bad side using positive actions. It helps us to look at different perspectives on a particular issue or generally about life. For instance, you do not go out partying every weekend just to look good with your peers, there are people your age who do not drink alcohol and party every weekend, but are still they are good. Therefore, if you do not have money to party every weekend, only do it when you have it; be real and face the challenges rather than being fake to show goodness and have difficulties in dealing with your reality.

It is also important to be aware of how often you take responsibility for your actions. For instance, it is good to acknowledge that you have failed the exam because you did not read, and not because the questions were vague. It is always good to accept your failure, just as you accept the successes; when you win a contest, appreciate, and when you lose, appreciate without giving excuses. When it comes to relationship, do not always think that it is only the other party that has problems and need to change, be aware that, you can also be at fault, and if it is the case, be ready to accept your fault and make changes to correct it. This attitude helps in encouraging a healthy relationship with other people. When if it comes to workplaces or group work it is important to consider that every person has his or her own strength, and therefore, you cannot consider yourself as of more strength or more importance than the others. Sometimes we tend to prove to people that we are the strongest, the most superior, and we are always right, and others are weak, of low level or weak. We often do this not realizing that our misinformed thoughts can lead to difficulties in relating to the other people. Therefore, it is important to think of the good that you have as a person, but be aware that you also have weaknesses that may be seen in different situations. Understanding your weaknesses helps you to understand and appreciate what you cannot change and try to bring out the best of you. To maintain good interaction with the other people, also understand that you are not always the best, your idea is not always the best, and therefore give other people a chance.

Encouraging Rational Ideas

Your thoughts will always influence what you feel. If you want to do something and suddenly you think that it will not be successful, there is a possibility that you will not try it or become passive about it. If you think that you require help to do something, even if it is something you can do alone you shy aware from doing it unless you find help. If you want to join a new game and a thought that the team members will not as you strike you, there is a likelihood that you will change your mind. All these courses of actions are dependent on one's thoughts and beliefs, which means that what you think and constantly say to yourself cause negative or positive emotions about something or an idea. Therefore, to encourage positive emotions, you must get rid of any irrational thoughts and welcome rational ones. You can do this by first identifying the irrational thoughts and challenge the problems that lead to irrational thoughts to help you have a different view of things and eventually feel differently. You should constantly persuade yourself to leave the irrational thoughts and take up thoughts that are reasonable. The irrational thoughts include thoughts such as, "I should be loved by everyone for me to be a better person," "I cannot avoid being unhappy," "things must go the way I want." Such thoughts are full of demands, musts, and should, which are difficult to fulfill in all situations, and therefore they do not represent reality. Reality will tell you that things must not happen the way you want them to, and they must or should not be done in a certain way, and therefore, there is no need to beat yourself when things do not happen as you would like them to. It had its causes, and you can always improve it later. If you want to join a new football team, do not think that the team members might not like me. Leave everything to cause, and feel free to go through the experience with an open mind. If things go as you wanted, good for you, and if they do not, accept and if there is something you can do to change the situation, try it out. However, if it still cannot work out, then accept and move on.

Challenging irrational thoughts might not be easy, but you can try this, if an event happens, it is good to have several interpretations of the situation. For example, if someone comments on your body, saying that you are flabby, instead of feeling bad about it and assume that all people think that you are unattractive, you can have a different interpretation. You feel hurt; you can interpret the situation as, not everyone sees me as flabby, putting on some fat is not bad, that comment is good for a start to maintain desirable body size, the person might just be projecting his or her weight problems to me. All these interpretations can be better and helpful than thinking that everybody does not like your body size. Another example is that if a partner rejects you, you can say to yourself, "maybe I should try meeting new people, instead of thinking that you are not likable.

Adopting a New Lifestyle

Everyone can be assumed to know the reason why things happen the way they do in their life; no one lacks an explanation. This means that everyone is the author of his or her life, and you can always change your lifestyle whenever you like. When what we expect to happen changes or happens in the way we did not expect, it might lead to frustrations. To counter the results of what we expect to happen, happening contrary, you prepare yourself with a lifestyle change. For example, you do not like hanging out with people and interacting in public places because you think that people will notice how big you are and make fun of you. It is only a thought that is either true or false, but because you do not know the outcome, you can choose to change your lifestyle to suppress the negative thoughts. Instead of confining yourself indoors, you choose to be someone out-going. It is something that you are not used to but if you put energy into it. When you do an activity for more than two weeks, behaviorists say that the activity becomes a habit. In this case, the activity of outgoing instead of being reserved for more than two weeks results in a habit. After some time, you will have changed your lifestyle and the thought of what people will say about you when they see you in public escapes you. This is because you are used to being in public and what people say does not matter anymore.

This strategy is simple, just look at the better traits that you have and would like to be maintained, and look at the bad traits that you would like to replace, and those that you are replacing with. The new behavior chosen must have the potential of changing your thoughts positively, and first, you should take just as a role you are playing, and before you know it, it is in your system and changes the way of thinking and view of things or ideas. A better lifestyle can be chosen and people such as friends and relatives will start seeing a different person.

Intentional Exposure

The thoughts of having an unfair treatment or getting a negative outcome can lead one to shy away from trying out new activities or interacting with new people. These thoughts can be destroyed through intentional exposure, for example, a person who fears darkness is continuously exposed to it on several occasions until he or she changes the thought that darkness is dangerous and frightening. Negative thoughts like "everyone should love and appreciate me," can be changed through exposing yourself to people who do not love and appreciate you until, you change the thought, and replace it with a positive and more realistic thought that, "not everyone would like and appreciate me." The change of thought will help you engage in any activity that would require the opinion of other people, and not fear negative feedback.

The ancient Chinese writings say that, tore the cloth because you can mend it. It means that when you are trying to fix things and they are not working, go to the extreme end and tear it apart because it is easier to mend because it is like starting over again. If someone laughed at you because you gave out a wrong answer, and felt bad about it, try to increase the number of times you answer questions in a wrong way, and even if they laugh at you, it will have no effect on you, hence the negative thought that keeps you from answering questions will be destroyed. This strategy requires commitments that would need a clear plan that is intentional to be followed until the desired change of thought is acquired.

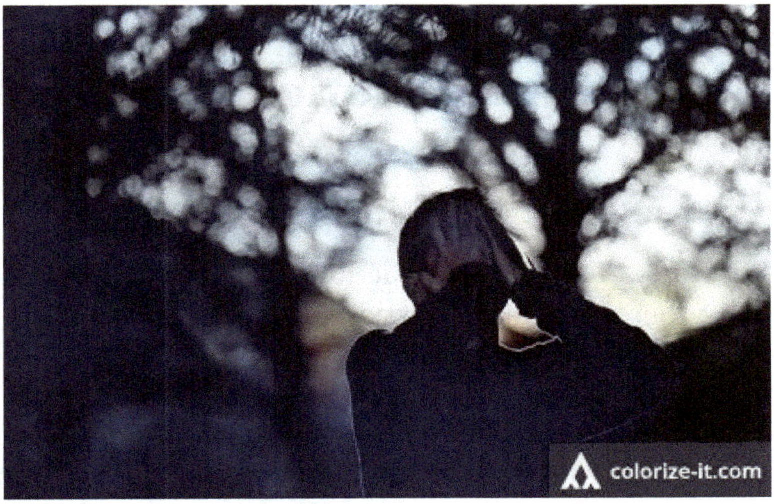
colorize-it.com

Chapter 5: Understand and Control Your Emotions

Understand Your Emotions

Emotions affect our daily interactions with other people and the way we perceive ideas or actions done to us. Emotions do not just occur; they are triggered by thoughts of an event in the present, past, or future. They are designed to communicate messages about the event that triggers them. When emotions are triggered, they seek attention to the things that are happening in our lives and the ones that will happen in the future or have already passed. For instance, when one experiences fear, it means that there is a threat to his or her life, and the person should act on the emotion by running away or acting on the danger. Sadness shows that you cannot get something you consider important or missed it and the reaction is an urge to stay alone, feel worthless. Emotions are considered negative or positive depending on the effect they have on a person; however, regardless of whether positive or negative, all emotions are important because they play an important role in our lives.

Emotions occur in the form of behavior shown through actions and urge; in our minds in the form of imaginations, memories, and thoughts; and body in the form of physical sensations. When we learn these three sets of manifestations, it is easy to understand emotions that we experience from time to time. Different emotions affect one's behavior, mind, and body in specific ways; for instance, when one feels angry, he or she is likely to increase heartbeat in the body, behave in a way to confront the situation that is causing anger, the mind starts thinking about the situation. This example shows that when we focus on the three aspects of our body that show emotions, it is easy to adjust to the emotions that we feel. It might not be an easy task to understand the specific emotions that you feel but with practice, you can get better. When one experiences fear, the mind is affected in a way that thoughts increases in the mind, and imaginations on what one can do also fills the mind or the mind can go blank depending on an individual. The body can show signs of rapid breathing, sweating, tensed muscles, and an increase in heart rate, among others. The behavior showed by the person can be avoidance of the situation, fight or run away, depending on the situation. When one feels contented, the mind focuses on what is bringing contentment; the body becomes calm and relaxed, and the person chooses to stay in the situation. Joy or happiness emotions make the mind think very fast focusing on the event that is bringing joy or happiness; the body becomes energized, and the behavior involves getting closer. Sadness has an effect on the mind in a way that the person focuses on the negative side of the situation and thinking slows down; the person feels body tiredness, numbness, empty and sometimes heavy; the affected individual is seen to be withdrawn. The emotions of guilt make the mind to focus on the criticizing self and concentrate on the opinion of other people; the body starts to sweat, the muscles are tensed, heart rate increases, the body feels tired and numb; guilt can make the one affected to hide from the situation and other people.

Learning your emotions and being aware of them is important because it helps survive or get along with the others. You should not let your emotions get in the way of good relations with other people. If the emotions are not correctly recognized and responded to, they get more intense with time and lead to destruction in our body; they can affect one's mental being and physical wellness. This is because the emotional message has not been read by the person affected and the feedback in terms of control has not been sent. It is either that the emotions have been suppressed, ignored, or misinterpreted such that anger is identified as fear. You should, therefore, have an emotional awareness in the sense that you can correctly name the emotions you are experiencing and explain them fully or partly. This is because you cannot act on something you do not know and know its characteristics. If you clearly know your emotions in a given situation, it is easy to recognize even when they start, and how they make you behave. You can also know how to describe them even when they are not shown in the behavior and body, remember it is not easy for another person to understand your emotions when they are only expressed in the mind.

Controlling Your Emotions

Controlling emotions is a competence that is required for survival and good social interaction. A person who is not able to control his or her emotions is likely to develop disorders such as depression, and developmental problems in social interaction. The control of emotions is not something that one is born with; it is learned through different kind of experiences from the society as a whole, teachers at school, friends, and parents. When children are born, they express themselves through emotions and it seems mostly when they cry. The crying calls for attention for them to be changed or fed. When they are happy, they also show it through smiles and giggles. The way the mother handles them helps them to have little knowledge of how to control their emotions, but it is always to a very small extent. As they continue with their growth, parents adopt ways of controlling the emotions of their children but it is always a short time strategy, in most cases, if they are negative emotions, they choose to suppress them by distracting them or avoiding them by ignoring them or threatening them. For instance, they are told that if they cry, they will be denied their toy. These methods of controlling the emotions work out for parents, as they slowly teach them that when you are sad or angry you do not react in that manner. When the children also interact with their peers during play, they acquire new skills on how to manage their emotions or strengthen what they have learned from the parents. However, sometimes it can get worse because they copy from each other. As the child grows up to adulthood, he or she must have developed his own ways of controlling emotions.

Apart from experience, emotions are also more expressed in certain individuals than in others. Some have good control while others do not have; this is attributed to the genetic makeup of an individual. In this case, we can say that all people experience emotions like anger, but the sensitivity varies from one person to another. The level of sensitivity can increase or reduced depending on the environment in which one is raised. For example, a person who was born with a high temper, if raised in an environment that encourages him or her to control his or her temper, the person is likely to have better control. Conversely, a person that is born with low temperament is likely to lack control if the environment does not offer guidance on control. It is important for a person to understand his or her emotions, in terms of are they more vulnerable or not so as to avoid situations that amplify certain emotions.

Controlling the emotions also differ in people because of the frequency one has experienced such emotions. For instance, a person who has frequently experience the loss of a loved one would manage emotions that come with a similar situation in the future than one who has experienced it less often. The prior experience becomes a teacher, and if the experience is repeated, the person becomes competent in controlling the emotions. Therefore, whenever you experience an emotion that is new to you, you should be more alert to see how it is expressed, and keep a record on how you control it; was the control method effective or not. The record helps incase the same emotion reoccurs, you know how to control and manage it. In addition, after experiencing the emotion, it is important to make choices on how you would react to it in the future.

For one to control emotions, he or she should have information on the limits of the emotions experienced reach; the highs and lows should be determined to make sure that when controlling you keep it within limits, also known as the zone of tolerance. The zone of tolerance is the area within the limit where the emotions can be controlled productively, depending on the intensity of the emotions. When the emotion reaches the higher limit, the person experiencing it is highly connected to the emotion, and therefore, he or she is overwhelmed to the extent that the control is limited and it becomes a hopeless situation. When it is on the lower limit, the person has little connection with the emotion, and therefore, it is difficult to recognize the emotion and connect to it. In this case, there is no reaction to the emotion because you cannot react to something you cannot recognize. In the zone of tolerance, the person is in control of the emotion, and therefore accepts and tolerates it. The person is capable of making decisions on how to react to the emotion. The individual also is capable of interacting with other people effectively, without the effect of the emotion. This is contrary to when a person is at the highest limit, where the intensity of the emotions is too high. Such a person cannot interact normally with the others because of the panic, feel anxious, and because it is difficult to slow the emotions, the person becomes impulsive, and his or her actions become irrational.

Depending on the level of vulnerability and emotional learning one has gone through, the ability to tolerate intense emotions is different. However, it is possible for everyone to come out of the zone of tolerance. Those faced more often with the emotions have mastered effective ways of staying within the zone of tolerance, and avoid getting to the lower and higher limits. Some people more often find themselves at either the lower or higher limit, and in most cases, they employ unhealthy strategies to cope with the situation. Therefore, it is important to keep track of all emotional reactions in order to maintain healthy reactions and keep away unhealthy reactions that let you out of the zone of tolerance.

Emotional reactions are the triggers of the emotions, the emotion, and the response to the emotion. In any emotional reaction, the trigger is always present, even if it is not seen or misunderstood, and the emotion is the exert feeling that has a label, for instance, anger. The response to the emotion is what varies from individual to another; some people become impulsive, which is seen in their sadness and aggression, while others result in self-harm. Both cases do not help the situation, and therefore, it is important to be aware of your emotions and recognize strategies that work well and those that do not work. For good control of emotions, it is better to change those reactions that do not work with the ones that work better for a particular emotion. You should also know when you are getting out of the zone of tolerance and when you are still in. after this, it is important to change reactions that do not work for the emotion and to achieve this you have to trigger the emotion and experiment on the new skill of managing it. Experiment with more new skills as you try out new resources that would make the situation better. The resources should help when the emotion is too intense or shut down. The chosen responses should be practiced to strengthen them as you expand the zone of tolerance. When the responses are strengthened, they become an automatic reaction when the emotion emerges, and with continued practice, you can become an expert in controlling your emotions within the tolerance limit, which allows you to interact with the other people without affecting them.

The most common negative emotions include frustrations, which occurs when someone is unable to move either back or forward. Frustrations can be caused by so many reasons, but the most important thing is to get rid of it or control it before it causes more negative emotions such as anxiety and anger. To deal with this emotion, you can think of something positive that can be tied to the situation, maybe those causing the frustration have their own good reason for doing so, and not to annoy you. The strategy helps you to find a way of looking at things differently, without negative thoughts. You can also remember any moment in the past that caused you frustration and how you worked it out perfectly. Just relax and try what worked out.

Nervousness, which is also referred to as anxiety is another negative emotion that can be controlled by breathing in deeply to slow down the heart rate. The focus should be on the breathing to help you get distracted from the situation that is causing anxiety. After breathing in and out slowly, now focus on something that will make the situation better. If what is making you nervous includes a series of things, write them down and commit time for each and how to deal with it. This will help you to come down because you now know that you are in control of the situation.

Another emotion is anger, which is the most destructive emotion. This emotion is mostly not handled well. Therefore, the signs of anger should be recognized early, and stop it before it begins. When anger is already started, it is good to stop everything and breathe deeply with the eyes closed. This strategy is to destruct the thoughts of anger and brings you back to positive thoughts. Another strategy is to look at yourself in the mirror and imagine how you would look like if your anger goes beyond what you are feeling at the moment. Imagine yourself shouting at everyone in the office, and how would you feel if you are the other party. This strategy brings you back on the positive track.

Disappointment is another negative emotion that brings the energy of a person down and makes one retreat from what is causing it. To deal with this emotion, remember that not everything will go as you plan or like; that is a reality that should be always in your mind. Therefore, just try another way out or amend your goal by either changing the deadline or changing the aspect that is hindering you from achieving your goal. If you have many things that are contributing to your disappointment record them in a notebook, and outline the steps that would help you to change the situation.

Emotions are very important as they help us deal with what needs our attention at the moment. Sometimes they can be overwhelming to the extent that they affect the way we react to situations. Therefore, for good utilization of emotions, one should be in control of them and maintain them in the zone tolerance, to ensure that we correct situations affecting us without interfering with our social interaction with the other people and maintain both physical and mental health.

Chapter 6: Overcoming Lack of Motivation: Strategies and Practical Tips

We first have to understand what motivation refers to in order to effectively learn how to overcome the lack of motivation. Motivation refers to the underlying aspect as to why people engage in various actions. The word motivation comes from the word motive. A motive is an insatiable want that requires satisfaction. They could be needs or desires that a person has grown over time. Generally, motivation is an innate feeling. This means that it is the feeling that you experience internally. A candid look at motivation and you will notice that this is what influences the behavior of a person. Behavior refers to the repetitive actions that an individual engages in. Motivation is what has made people move on from worse situations in life. It should be noted that motivation may originate internally or externally. This means that motivation is influenced by our subconscious and consciousness.

This chapter, however, is keen to focus on the lack of motivation that an individual's experience. As human beings, one of our shortcomings is that we tend to lack the motivation to engage in various activities. The activities mentioned above might be very remote or it might be something that has been haunting you all your life. Almost everyone in life has found themselves in this situation. Lack of motivation is not a permanent state and thus it can be overcome. If we stay positive and motivated in life, we tend to achieve more. You have a subtle time doing something because you lack motivation. There are various causes of lack of motivation and they include;

Causes of Lack of Motivation

Falling Below the Threshold

We all desire to be engaged in a particular activity. What makes the difference is what we are doing about it Lack of motivations sprouts from procrastination. This is the desire to do something but the feeling of delay arrests you on the way. Many people who are actively engaging in different activities will tell you that they had no motivation at the onset of the activity. They began the activity on solid ground and now they are making it happen. This is a pointer to many individuals who lack motivation, sometimes you have to let go of the feeling of laziness and take up an activity even if you are not feeling it. Motivation will find you on the way.

Look at a scenario where an individual decides to relax on the couch the whole day. He or she may be deeply engraved in the television or it may be some other activity that does not require motion. At the end of the day, this kind of person will feel tires yet he or she has literally done nothing. The stationery activity that we were engaging in has drawn a lot of energy from our bodies. Now there is this different scenario where you have had a packed day. You had a series of activities and you were able to move from one task to another expeditiously. Motivation is either cultivated or destroyed. When you feel like you do not want to engage in a particular activity, you ought to change this notion because cultivating motivation comes from doing the exact opposite of what we want to do. When we engage in these activities that we do not want, motivation picks up on the way and you will find that you engage in these events aptly once you commence.

Feeling of Depression

When we are depressed, all our energies and focus are channeled into our feelings. This way our motivation escapes us. Going through various tasks of the day can be subtle when you are depressed. Sometime you will find yourself building castles in the air due to what is affecting you. When this happens, your attention shifts from the task you are engaging in the thoughts of depression and this way we find ourselves making mistakes at our place of work. You find yourself not struggling so much to get through your tasks because you have the "don't care" feeling in you.

Depression can be countered by talking to a therapist. This is an expert who is in a position to orchestrate the best action plan for you. With a therapist, you are able to trace your path of recovery. When depressed, we can counter a lack of motivation by deciding in our minds and prioritizing the things that come as the most important first. If you are a musician with the art of playing an instrument, that instrument plays a huge role as a stress reliever. There are a number of things that are fatally important despite the depression that you might be experiencing. For instance, you are supposed to pay various bills in order to continue enjoying the services that you have been enjoying. Depression can be overcome by the celebration of the miles you move no matter how minute.

Confusion and Overwhelm

This results when you have too much on your plate that you feel you are not in a position to digest. Lack of motivation sprouts from the feeling of having nothing to do as earlier on discussed but motivation can also be destroyed when you have a lot of things to accomplish in that you feel like you may not be in a position to achieve the objectives. As a result, you have a feeling of letting go. When you feel like your schedule will not accommodate what you want to do comprehensively, you might be drawn back and not even want to engage in the activity at all.

When you are going through this setback, one should consider the fragmentation of tasks into particles that you can easily digest. This means that you divide your tasks into smaller portions that we can easily accomplish. Break the task into various portions for instance. Going to school will require apt preparations in that you do not want to miss anything while in school. In order to achieve this task, you can break it into doing your assignment, preparation, and traveling.

Pleasing Everyone

We all have an understanding of who people-pleasers are. These are individuals who want to gain fame by pleasing everyone. Research has it that this kind of people lack motivation because they actually do not know what they want to do. When you do not know what you want to do, you will not have the motivation to do it. People pleasers have the motivation to please people which carries them only half of the way. When their bid to please people is satisfied, they are left in a vacuum not knowing what to do. Most of the time you would not know how to get over it on your own.

It is almost hilarious to say that you are motivated to achieve other people's goals. Having your own goals help a great deal to boost your motivation. When you do not feel motivated, this could be because you are trying to please everyone. When your focus is on trying to please everyone, most of the time you will find that the resulting effect is letting yourself down constantly. This is because you will never be in a position to please everyone to the latter.

A Fixed Mindset

A fixed mindset is one that makes you have the perception that you are not in control of mostly what happens. You have placed yourself in a constraint in that you tell yourself you cannot accomplish some things. You are not certain with your abilities whatsoever. This way you look down upon yourself. You tell yourself that you cannot engage in various activities due to your shortcomings. It may be in sports for instance whereby you look at yourself and tell yourself you cannot engage in a particular type of sport due to various reasons that are in-born.

When you have this type of perception, you are not motivated to change the status quo of things because after all, you tell yourself you are not in a position to do so. You do not invest your time in trying to accomplish new things because you believe it is pointless. In order to walk away from this type of mindset, you need to adopt a mindset that allows you to grow. This way you are able to view life as having numerous opportunities in which you can engage in. You are able to welcome critiques and work on your shortcomings.

Contentment

This is a feeling that you are satisfied with what you have and that you do not require further input in order to achieve anything else. Contentment is a value that should be appreciated although in most cases, it has been seen to be a causation factor of lack of motivation. Your mind is tuned to a default setting whereby you believe that you have everything you require. With this perception at hand, you do not want to work to achieve new things. The realization that things might need to change is what helps a great deal when trying to change this mindset.

How to Overcome Motivation

By the sense of our natural existence, it is normal that we will be more motivated in some days as compared to others. This is what brings about the equilibrium of life. Most of the time, your mood has had a direct effect on your motivation. This can be countered through resting and relaxing. When you want to overcome your lack of motivation, you will have to go deeper to the roots to find out its causes in order to know how to counter it. Having the basic knowledge of the causes of lack of motivation as aforementioned, we will now embark on what are the strategies to overcome this state.

Focusing on the Prize

We all have set goals in our lives. The ones that act as a driving factor to what we engage in. Over time, we tend to lose sight of what is key in our lives. This happens as a result of being so deeply engraved in the pressures of trying to make ends meet in life. Owing to this, our focus shifts from our main goals and this is what takes a toll on our motivation. We often change the perception of how we look at the activities that we have been engaging in. Often you will find that you feel tired doing these tasks.

For you to regain your motivation, you need to ask yourself why you are engaging in a particular activity and is that activity a stepping stone towards achieving your goals. With this pointer in place, you are able to make headway. You can also prioritize your activities and in so doing you evaluate the gravity of what you are engaging in versus your life. Make sure that you always have your dreams at heart. In so doing, you will know that you have a bigger purpose than you might be thinking. Due to the changing times, you ought to re-evaluate your goals. This will help you in staying on course towards achieving your goals.

Input Where You Work

There are various factors that might come as limiting when it comes to your work. It may be a pinching chair, it may be the lighting or even the set up that is not working for you. Changing this situation will see to it that your perception changes, when your perception changes, you can function more effectively. This increases your motivation to work. For instance, prolonged use of particular equipment may lead to monotony. Monotony comes with boredom which has a negated effect on your motivation. There are many types of equipment that might work for you especially in the work set up. Pictures of your relatives and family play a huge role in a bid to increase motivation. This way you are reminded why you work so hard. This also personalizes your workspace and makes you feel at home when you are working.

Have a Vision of Success?

Before engaging in a task, your brain tends to form an estimate on how long it will take to complete the task and how many obstacles you might encounter. This way you are able to have a predetermined perception of success or failure. In order to hype your motivation when engaging in a particular task, you are to adopt a perception of success. This way the mind and the body will follow suit. When visualizing every step of your task from start to stop, you are in a position to enjoy your success even before you attack the task and this way, you can easily accomplish the task.

Fragment Your Tasks

Fragmentation of tasks refers to the division of tasks into smaller tasks that are easily available. This is in a bid to help counter a huge task gradually. You probably have various tasks throughout the day, it may vary according to intensity. There are some tasks that are overwhelming in nature in that the thought of completion escapes your mind and wind of lack of motivation arrests you.

You have difficulty in accomplishing numerous tasks then it is only fair to consider having a list in which you will use to cross-check all the activities that you ought to accomplish on a particular day. This aids in not leaving out any task and keeps you on course. You ought to keep updating your checklist since the busy schedule might be complex in nature.

Objectify Your Goals

This is a technique that focuses on the rewarding of oneself for the miles that you may have moved. The technique has gained a lot of fame due to its reflection of the gaming world. Owing to this it has been referred to as gamification. Just like in the gaming world, gamification entails that you reward yourself for the various steps you keep achieving. In this manner, you are able to keep track of your path through your obstacles. This also keeps your motivation at top-notch.

Routine Change

We take part in various activities throughout the day. When this happens, we are inclined to face boredom. This is because of the monotony that builds up as a result of the same. Changing the routine of what happens in your life plays a big role in making sure that you stay motivated. You change the way you look at your tasks, you are able to move through your tasks with ease. A routine change also makes sure that you focus keenly on every aspect of your work. You are able to accord your work with various timelines that fit your routine. Here you engage your work more actively.

Creating motivation is often easy. What creates an uphill task is staying motivated. People have the motivation to pick up a task but what defeats them is staying keen on the task. Creating a culture of supportive environment will see to it that you remain motivated. Have someone that keeps on checking on you in order to remain on course.

Chapter 7: How to Think Positive in Your Everyday Life to Reach Your Goals

As social beings of nature, we are influenced by the waves of positivity and negativity. This is a representation of our cognition. Our cognitive mind is made up of thoughts that influence us the way we think and respond to various stimuli. This chapter focuses on the positive side of our cognition. How positivity may affect our general achievements. It is not a myth that positive-minded people have a way of getting through their lives more smoothly.

Positive thinking entails the process of an individual directing his or her thoughts to the wave of positivity. Normally, this process results in the effect of general happiness, success, and a sense of belonging. This type of individual is able to go over any obstacle with lesser effects on the emotional quotient. Many people have viewed this type of topic as being nonsense and of no inner meaning. This is because they do not respond to it positively. In the recent past, a study has shown that there is a growing number of individuals who have begun to accept this kind of perception. They have adopted the wave of positive thinking and it seems to be working to them at every instance in life. Positivity has been a subject that has proven to gain popularity.

Numerous amounts of the book have been writing about this topic. Research has it that a lot of people are seeking to find out what this is. In order to bring about the use of this type of perception in your life, you need to have an in-depth look at this topic. The topic runs deeper than just the definition. You have to embrace positive thinking and use it to your advantage in order to understand its benefits.

The Wheel of Positive Thinking

To explain how positive thinking operates, I am going to use the help of various scenarios. Take this example of Robert who applies for a job vacancy at Money plots May Bach. Due to Robert's negativity, he believes that the probability of him getting the job is next to zero. Robert looks down on himself as being a failure. Due to this negated wave, Robert has the belief that other applicants seeking the same vacancy are better placed than him. This is what influences his thoughts of failure. This is what runs through Roberts's mind the whole week before the interview. He has no thoughts of success whatsoever.

On the day of the interview, he wakes up late and finds out that the garments he was to put on are dirty and furthermore he has no supplies in the house to cook breakfast. The negativity has already caused him three jeopardies that are going to follow him throughout the day. He proceeds to work with the wrinkled clothes and o an empty stomach. At the interview, the earlier factors come to life. His empty stomach is growling all the time due to hunger. He is tensed due to his phobia of under qualification. He is also anxious that his wrinkled clothes might be noticed. With all this in mind, Robert is distracted to the extent that his attention is taken away haphazardly.

Another character applied for the same job. Kim approached his situation calmly and maturely.He was sure that the interview would be challenging but his mind was focused on how he would get through the interview. He knew that there are other applicants nevertheless he believed in himself as being the best. Before the interview, Kim spends most of his time creating a picture in his mind that all is going to be well and that he is going to make it in the interview. This is because he believed in himself. Due to this approach, Kim took time to prepare the evening before the interview. He took to sleep early because he knew that he had to be prepared for the task ahead of him. On a fateful day, he woke up on time and made sure that he had his breakfast and was ready to depart. He arrived at the destination even before time. All these were contributing factors that led to a cultivation of a good impression at the job.

From the two stories, we can deduce a few things. Mindset is key in whatever we engage in. We need to approach every stage in our lives in a manner that suggests we are ready to learn from them. Everything in a natural manner will favor you when you tend to approach it calmly and warmly.When we have a positive attitude, we tend to elicit endorphins that have a positive response in making us feel more inclined to happiness. We have more energy to engage in various activities since we appreciate the attributes of our bodies more often. The key effect of positive thinking is our bodies. We think positively, our bodies respond positively, we become healthier.

Our environment affects us in various ways. Some are more complex than we can imagine. The way we behave for instance is a reflection of the people we have interacted with and the experiences that we have been through. You will often find an individual who is negated to relate this feeling to an event that took place in the past in his life. Positive people follow the path of positivity that may have been initiated at some point in their life. It is a normal concept that we tend to be attracted to positive individuals than negative ones. The study has it that positive people tend to relay some positivity to us. This is the same thing with negative people in that you will find negative people relaying their negativity to you. Absolutely nobody would want to be unhappy or associate themselves with feelings that make them feel frustrated. When you are positive, you are most likely to stumble upon help. People confirm the veracity of this by extending a sense of likeability towards people who are positive.

In life, thinking negatively will always have a negative effect on your plans. Your set objectives will not be met once you adopt thinking that is negated. In order to achieve your goals, you need to adopt a mindset that will help you move through all the obstacles and ensure that at the end of the day you are able to emerge. There are a number of strategies that when adopted, play an important role in making you change the way you view various instances and make sure that you emerge. The various strategies work best when they are done in repetition. The practice is always the best way we can achieve perfection.

How to Shift the Wave to Positivity in Order to Achieve Your Goals

Do Not Exaggerate

We tend to express feelings about ourselves now and then. This is because we are true to self and we seek to achieve an honest analysis of ourselves. Take for instance when we are saying about our behavior that has defined us in the past. It may be negative, yes but saying it positively will make it sound better. You may be saying "I have always disliked public gatherings" This is a negated expression towards public gatherings. When an individual expressed, they are feeling this way, it has the effect of making the situation remain constant and not change for the better. When you say "I have always disliked public gatherings but this situation is going to change" this gives room for your mindset to adopt another outlook towards this subject. Sticking to one mindset and avoiding flexibility is often what makes individuals adopt a negated outlook towards life.

Block Negativity

In this realm, we have to appreciate the fact that negativity will always manifest itself everywhere and anywhere. In order to survive, we need to adopt mechanisms that will allow us to shield ourselves from the negativity that exists all around us. When we do this, we give room for positive thoughts to prevail. When positive thoughts prevail, we are able to achieve whatever we desire in our lives.

Often than sooner, we find ourselves drowning in the wave of negativity. When this happens, we need to immediately discover the turn of events and adopt mechanisms that will aid you in regaining the flow of positive thoughts that existed before this change. When the reality check we give to ourselves exceeds the limits, it now shifts to insults that we give to ourselves. The same way we would stop an individual from giving insults to another is the same way that we ought to prevent ourselves from insulting ourselves.

Elicit the Positive

When you block the negative, there is room left to exhibit the positive. Love is at the core of positivity since showing a sense of kindness towards oneself is one step towards making sure that you embrace positivity. Most writers on love relate it to the sense of looking for the good in everything. It is only when you see the good that you will start to show positivity towards it. You could have gone for an interview and not gotten the job but you tried and gave it your best. The way you visualize every ounce in your life will have a resulting effect on how you function and operate. You could have played a rugby match and lost. How you get up from that loss and focus on the next match is what will determine if you are going to win those subsequent matches.

Embrace It

You have the anxiety of being at a social gathering, what you need to do is embrace it rather than letting it eat you up. Blow it off. Shake it off anything you may do in order to keep you going. Remember sticking to specific events is what generates the feelings that we don't like. You have been embarrassed in front of the class, do not shy off, embrace it, and channel it. You can use this as a platform for asking numerous questions in a bid to better your understanding. Generally, the more positive outlook you according to a situation, the better position you are at success in moving from it.

Let Go

Yes, there are some instances that you might have brought shame to yourself. This does not have to define you. You do not have to keep reminding yourself about these events. You can take time and let them flow through your body. When they leave your body, you should not allow them to affect you again. Understand that you have no control over the events of the past. Exactly as the name suggests they are past your control. Reminding yourself of the instances where you went wrong has an effect of making you feel like you are bullying yourself. You hurt yourself too much when you are recurrently reminding yourself of your failures in life. You do more justice to your body and feelings by just accepting that the events took place the way they did. This way you have a remedial approach when you encounter the same situation again. People who draw negativity from a situation have the problem of encountering it for the second time. They would probably respond the same way or even worse to the same situations.

Motivate

Focusing on the positive will have an effect of making sure that you are always motivated to take up various tasks and events in your life. You have a level of confidence that allows you to be self-contented when taking up a particular task. You are constructive in your thinking. The constructive perspective of thinking has been seen to bring a solution to problems rather than complicate them more. Motivation is as basic as a monologue. Talk to yourself and tell yourself that you can achieve it. When the desire to achieve is cultivated, we tend to have that passion that will lead to success. We experience various successes in our lives, it could be as minimal and remote as it may be. It could be something significant in your life. When we achieve various successes, we ought to make sure that we extend a sense of congratulations towards ourselves. Many people ignore this but, in most cases, it has been seen to bring about a lot of change. The art of congratulations can be a stepping stone from one success to another.

Remaining Positive

In one way or another, you will find that we commit mistakes in our lives. It could be to ourselves or others. We commit a mistake to others and adopt a restrictive mindset will not be of any aid to you. Accept that you have made a mistake, apologize for it, and learn how you can move from it. There are some people who tend to be apologetic all of the time. Most of their conversations are filled with remorseful sentiments. A person who would take account for something that he might not have done. This type of perception towards interactions is not advisable since negated people may take advantage of this.

Self-Responsibility

You owe no one your responsibility. We are not omnipotent in nature so that we control everything that takes place in our lives. Everything happens as an act of God. You do not have to face the consequences of events that you did not orchestrate. This means that when you are extending your help to people, you ought to do it to a degree that does not have an effect on you. The feeling that you need to see the occurrence of everything and anything should be eradicated. You offer help where you cannot where you must. Other people should be responsible for their actions and not you. No one has the power to influence changes in another person's emotions. Trying to change the way an individual feel is a complete waste of energy and resources. The feeling is mutual. You are responsible for your own happiness. You will encounter the feeling of guilt, you will be overwhelmed, and some people will even look down upon you. You have to take control of your body and emotions in order to make sure that you do not respond in a manner that is disrespectful to your friends.

Accept Compliments and Critic

Often you will be told congratulations about various successes that you might have achieved in your life. This should not go to your head. Chanel, this to be your motivating factor. Do not dwell too much on previous successes but focus on the next. This is how you will build yourself. When cruise, on the other hand, do not let it go to your heart, accept critic welcome it, use it to modify yourself into the best model you can be. Positive criticism has often brought about positive change. We should thus welcome criticism when it comes.

Chapter 8: Practical Strategies to Overcome Fear

Holding on to fear means that a person has lost control of their bravery. A person who holds on to fear has no courage to fight for what they want in life, and also a fearful person does not take risks. They are afraid of starting again because fear controls their life. It is essential for a person to overcome fears so that one can achieve their life goals. However, there are several facts about the fear that people do not know. Before focusing on how to get rid of fear, it is useful first to know these facts.

Facts About Fear

- Fear is reasonable, and every normal person goes through fear. When going through anxiety, sometimes a person might think that they are weak because they believe they are going through a dull phase. However, even the brave has fears. Lack of fear could be a problem in the brain.

- Fear comes in different forms for different people. While for some people, fear comes from anticipation for others, it may be different. There is, however, no small fear because different people handle different things. That one is afraid of something you think is petty does not make them weak. That is their fear, and it does not define them.

- Fears are not just natural; some are formed along in life while others are forced on others by people. Natural fears are happening as a result of normal emotions like sadness. Fears that are formed later in life could be from bad experiences we have gone through, and therefore we are afraid to do something because we have been through it and it left us hurt. Forced fears happen from how hearing the people we trust to talk about things, and we believe. Some people, for example, believe snakes are demons and teach this to their children and therefore due to these teachings, the children end up fearing all snakes.

- Fears sometimes are imaginary and not a reflection of what is our reality. For example, some people fear aliens even when there has never been a real identified alien. We imagine things and believe them, therefore, causing us fear.

- The more you focus on your fears, the more the fears tend to look real. If you are always scared of something, it might become more real that you end up losing grip on your reality. If you think by walking in the dark, you will see a ghost; you are most likely to see images of ghosts in front of you even when there is no real ghost.

- Fears are major determinants of what we will do. Fears are sometimes intuitions in that if your anxiety tells you not to go somewhere, you are unlikely to go there. Fear will make a person resign from their job because they fear being fired when the bosses had no such thoughts. Fears always direct someone in making various decisions.

- The greater your fear, the greater the damage you are likely to impact on yourself. This is because fear accumulates so rapidly if not dealt with. Someone may be so afraid of a medical result, get very stressed from having to wait and think it's taking too long because it will be a bad result. Since they already feel the results are bad, they might even commit suicide before the results come.

It is for these reasons why it is important to get rid of all fears, small or big. But since fear is normal, then controlling some fears which could others grow into a mountain of fear.

Ways of Overcoming Fear

- Identifying the fear is the step towards overcoming fear. What makes you afraid, and why does it make you afraid. Where does the fear come from, and what led to this fear? Sometimes we are carrying the fear of the unknown, and hence it becomes hard to fight it. To fight something, you have first to know what it is.

- Look at the implications of the identified fear. What does it prevent you from doing? Has the fear made you lose touch of your reality? Has fear made you lose touch with your loved ones? How much more are you likely to lose if you keep holding on to the fear?

- Be curious about what instigates your fear. What thoughts, events, or people awaken your fear? In doing this, you can learn how to avoid or deal with these sources of your fear. Without knowing the cause of your fear, it is difficult to let go of the fear.

- Focus on the present instead of the unknown future. Sometimes the worry about tomorrow will only make your fears grow more. Trying to solve fear each new day may yield more success than trying to fight unknown. Every day will have its worry and dealing with each at a time will prevent an accumulation of the same, which will be harmful in the long run.

- Have something that can distract you from your fears. Whenever the first feeling of fear strikes, it's important to have a distraction because sometimes focusing on fear will increase it. The distractions could include pinching yourself back into reality or any other distraction that could alert you when it's time to do something else for distraction.

- Encourage positivity when negativity strikes. When amidst your fear, try to think of something good, something that will counter the fear and something that will fight the negativity out. Fear can be contained by self-motivation that comes from positive thinking. Look at that thing you are afraid of and think of how brave you are how much you overcome in the past, and you will find the fear fading off.

- Be grateful in everything; acknowledge everything you are thankful for. If you are a manager and always have a fear of failing your bosses or juniors, be thankful that you got the opportunity others are always looking for. Be thankful that you hold a unique feature that made you the boss and not others.

- Having a well-kept record of your fears will ease the struggles of trying to identify them. A record will help you note the fears you are about to deal with and also help realize the ones you have already dealt with so that you can observe how far you have come. A record may even encourage you when you look at big fears you have managed to overcome in the past.

- Speak out your fears. Sometimes we are afraid to voice out our fears, and this magnifies the fear. Talking about it may help you realize that what you are holding on to is not as big as you perceive it. Talking about it will also allow others who have gone through the same thing or have extensive knowledge to help you out. You won't get help unless you take the first initiative of talking about it and letting others help you out.

- Sometimes seeking help from a profession is very important. Our family and friends may lend us a listening ear, but if they haven't gone through the same thing, they may not be of much help. A person who has gone through it might help you by introducing you to their way, but sometimes what works for others might not work for you. A professional will you identify your way so that it works perfectly for you.

- Learn how your mind works so that you can fight away your fears. By learning this, you will get to know your thought patterns so that it becomes easier to avoid negative thoughts before they strike. Avoiding negativity is an excellent remedy to escape your fears. After all, prevention is better than cure.

- Find motivation in books and other people's experiences about the fear you are struggling with. To learn more about your fear, you need to look at it from other people's perspectives. You may learn something new about your fear you never existed.

- Face your fears because unless you do, you will never get rid of them. Avoiding your fears will only work for a short time, but if you need a long-term solution, you have to deal with it. Fight it and terminate it completely so that the problem is gone once and for all.

- If afraid of talking to friends or even a profession, the good thing is that these days there is everything online. Watch something online that will talk about your fear, and it could greatly help you.

- Sometimes what you eat has a lot to do with your feelings. Make sure to eat food that gives you good energy avoiding all the sugar rush and chemicals that might lead to negative energy. Have a proper diet that helps you get good energy and hence no room for negativity.

- Look at things in a different view and stop overthinking. Letting your mind always have a bad attitude towards situations will raise your fear more. It is important to change your perspective on all issues so that you kick out all the negativity that brings you fear.

- Learn to adapt to what you cannot change. Sometimes trying to change something beyond our means will only increase our fears. You are not always going to be able to control everything, let go of what is beyond you, and focus on what you can.

- Believe in yourself because sometimes what you are afraid of is just in your mind. You may have a fear that people don't like you while people don't feel that way about you. Believe in yourself and your impact on people. Instead of focusing on your flaws concentrate on the good you do to others and the influence you have on people.

- Learning that not everything will always go our way will help get rid of your fear. Sometimes the fear is out of thinking that we could fail. Accept the possibilities of failure so that you don't have anything else to fear. Accept that anything could go wrong and get rid of the fear of that happening. This means accepting the worst that could happen in all situations even before it happens.

- Make a move in fighting the fear by doing things you are afraid of. Are you afraid of talking to someone because you regard them so highly? Go and speak to them. The person you are afraid of might even be more accommodating than you could have ever imagined. If you are afraid of tackling a specific project because you are worried you cannot handle it, do it, try and you might end up surprising yourself.

- Learn from your fear because everything is a learning experience. Learn the strategy that helped you get rid of the fear because you never know when you might need it. Learn how to avoid it and even importantly learn who you can count on.

- Get a person who you can emulate. Someone who went through a similar experience and came out successful in overcoming the fear you are going through. Such a person will motivate you when you are about to give up or when you think that everything is too much for you to handle.

- Seek spiritual guidance when everything else is not working. Spirituality comes along way in helping us deal with our fears. Pray and meditate because that might be where your solutions lie.

- Think ahead of the worst that could happen in your given situation and tell yourself that even if it happens, you will still be happy. Learn to motivate yourself that a single situation will not determine your happiness. Accept things ahead of time and brace yourself for any possibility.

- Some energy of fears is best released by doing yoga. The breathing in and out will help the release and intake of negative and positive energy.

- Identify the purpose of your fear. Sometimes fear is not bad because it helps you be ready for something worse happening in your life. It is great to know what the purpose of your fear is and work on it. If this means taking precautions before doing something, make sure to be cautious because your fear might help you avoid a bad outcome.

- Deal with the fear of failure by accepting that as a human; you are bound to fail sometimes. Most of our fears are based on fear of failure, especially when a person perceives their worth regarding how much they achieve or lose. A person's value goes beyond their failures because the effort of trying also counts. Most successful people in life have, at some point, failed. Some may have more than you know, but they rose from the fear and forged on. So, do not be afraid because of the many times you have failed, always pick yourself up fight the fear of failure.

- Go down the memory lane of your fears and find the constant fear you always drop but somehow always pick back up again. Observe why it recurs and where you go wrong in eliminating it. Find an excellent strategy to get rid of it finally.

- Having a good breath sometimes is the magic in overcoming fear. When you allow yourself to have a good inhale of fresh air, it will relax your mind and body and help the fear escape out of your system. This is very effective, especially for someone who is about to do public speaking but is afraid of a large crowd. By letting in a good breath of air, the fear goes away, and they can confidently address people.

- Identify the emotions that provoke your fears. Sometimes sadness will cause so much fear of already past situations or even make you afraid of facing something else that will make you sad. Identifying the emotions that worsen your fears will help you work hard to avoid them and therefore avoiding fear all the same.

- Invest your time in doing something that will make you forget your fears. Instead of sitting around and worrying or focusing on the worry, take time off and get busy with something more engaging and one that is unlikely to remind you of what you are running away from.

- Strive to always attract positive energy because with the positivity around you; there is no room for fears. Your fears are eventually determined by the energy you possess.

- Forgive yourself for all the things you blame yourself for. Sometimes you are afraid of giving yourself second chances because you blame yourself for failing the first time. Truth is not everyone gets it right the first time. If you think you always try and fail, forgive yourself and promise to find other ways to go about situations instead of holding grudges for yourself. Holding on to these grudges against yourself often leads to fear of trying again, or taking future risks. You will find so much freedom from fear when you let go of things that brought your fear. If you were given a task at work and did not deliver in time, don't hold that, and think you are slow. This will only give fear of taking another project because you think you will be late again.

Chapter 9: Overcoming Anxiety and Depression

Anxiety creates a state of helplessness in a person as someone struggles with the fear of the unknown. Anxiety is almost impossible to solve by ourselves, and we need help from professionals from time to time. The use medically treats some types of anxieties of drugs to help calm a person down. Anxiety will most often lead to depression because of the severe impact of anxiety in a person. Here we are going to look at how anxiety and depression can both be eliminated by positive thinking.

It is essential to know the symptoms of someone going through anxiety and depression so that it is easier to help them out if they are our family and friends. We may also be struggling with the two without knowing that it is anxiety and depression. Here is how to tell so that we can also help ourselves in time before it ultimately damages us.

Signs of Anxiety and Depression

- A person struggling with the two usually loses all interest they had. It could be somebody who loved singing and would sing at any given a chance, but they now stop singing, and even when forced to they will still refuse to participate.

- There will a change in their eating. They will either start overeating than they usually did or even stop eating at all only eating very little when they previously had a very high appetite.

- The two also brings about loss of memory even on new things that are unlikely to be forgotten. A person will also find it hard to pay attention to someone in a conversation, and even making decisions on matters becomes too hard.

- Someone will also start experiencing physical problems like constant headaches and fatigue due to constant worrying.

- A person with anxiety and depression is like to have a sleeping disorder such as lack of sleep or too much sleep. Sometimes they can stay up all night and still not sleep during the day and sometimes they can sleep during the day and throughout the night.

Negativity often causes someone to feel hopeless and helpless and therefore leading to anxiety and depression. Anxiety will develop due to excessive stress brought by negative thinking. Negative thinking also causes low self-esteem, and without self-esteem, one has no belief in their ability to overcome the two. Having positive thinking will heal you as a person and give you the bravery to overcome anxiety and depression.

One can start with positive affirmations that defeat the negativity that leads to anxiety and depression. These affirmations can help reduce all the symptoms of anxiety and depression and even wholly heal the whole thing when taken seriously. Affirmations also help people are already on the road to recovery. These are how affirmations work when you believe in the positive affirmations and in their ability to change you as a person; the affirmations are highly likely to yield positive results for you.

Ways of Creating Positive Affirmations

The following points are meant for a person who is struggling through anxiety and depression to come up with affirmations that will help them. When a person absorbs each of these points and internalizes them, they should then come with simple affirmations understood in their perfect understanding.

1. Love yourself without any limits whatsoever.
2. Believe in your strength and say it over and over to yourself.
3. Allow yourself to only deal with other positive-minded people.
4. Believe in the favored life has accorded you and trust that you have the very best for you at that moment.
5. Be happy and everyone around you. Do not allow the two to steal your joy, so adapt where necessary.
6. Focus on what makes you joy instead of putting all your energy on negativity.
7. Enjoy every moment at a time and quit worrying about what will happen the next moment.
8. Have a positive attitude towards your problems. Look at your issues as a learning opportunity instead of looking at it as another problem specially molded for you.
9. Allow yourself positive energy as you eventually become a product of your energy.

10. Believe in your ability to control your thinking. Do not sit and think you are helpless. Think of the most amazing things you can achieve for yourself instead.

11. Love everything about you and what you own. Do not despise anything about yourself as it will make your fears rise. Do not also dislike any of your family or friends or possession as this will make you more resentful and anxious.

After going through these points and coming up with strong affirmations, one is supposed to implement them. The success will be determined by how frequently and hard you practice them. You could achieve better success by standing in front of a mirror every day and reading yourself the affirmation. The more you read, the more you can believe in them. And the more you believe in the affirmations, the more likely they are to work for you.

It may be difficult during the first stages of the practice, but as time goes by, everything becomes easier and more achievable. Write the affirmations in the first-person sentences will help the affirmations sound more believable.

As you recite your affirmations, it is good to make sure you are replacing your negative energy with the new positivity. Where there was negativity cancel it and put positivity as this will help in eventually forgetting or getting rid of the negativity. Whenever you feel like the affirmations are not working for you, sit back and reflect on the goals you want to eventually achieve as this will help motivate you to push on. Sometimes you will look at your goals, and they may seem too ambitious, affirm yourself that they are achievable and set them more reasonably. This may include writing them down and working to achieve them from the most important or most urgent so that you are saved of time and also so that you can see your progress.

Meditate on your affirmations; there is something magical about having a meditation on this because you can imagine how it will be for you after you achieved them. You can imagine that they have already worked out for you and that you are already at your happy place. See how much that will make you feel and believe the results of following through your affirmations will be as you imagined it.

Place your affirmations at every in every yet private place that you can always see. Make them available for you at every single point you are likely to be alone so that when you see them, you can remember what you are doing.

Do not give up even when you think that the affirmations are not working as fast as you would wish them. Results are different for every person, and if yours are taking longer, you should not put them away at all for that. Continue working through them and believe that in no time and when you are ready, you will see the results.

There are many advantages associated with positive thinking as a remedy for anxiety and depression. Some of these include:

- Positive thinking is a strategy you can use on your own without any help from people. This is important because when it just involves you, you have a say on when, where, and how it will take place instead of waiting for others to decide for you or waiting for others to avail themselves.

- Positive thinking helps you avoid any medication that would have otherwise been used without mindfulness therapy. And honestly, it would be best to avoid medication if there is another better remedy.

- It's affordable for everyone as it does not involve anyone investing their money. Therefore, it is a remedy for both the rich and the poor and also helps a person gain control over their own decisions.

Positive thinking has been attributed to very many great things that are also the reason why it is much recommended for anxiety and depression. But some will ask why positive thinking. What impact does positive thinking have?

Advantages of Positive Thinking

Positive thinking allows someone to lead a long, happy life, and happiness is very important in dealing with anxiety and depression. A happy person is unlikely to have anxiety problems and therefore, no depression.

Positive minded people are unlikely to have depression because they live each day and moment at a time. They are likely to talk about their issues more than an unhappy person.

Positive thinking reduces the likelihood of stress because positivity means not holding on to things that deprive you of your peace. Therefore, if a person is peaceful, they are less stressed and thus no likelihood of developing anxiety.

Positive thinking makes a person healthy psychologically and physically and therefore, able to deal with anxiety and depression when it strikes.

Positive thinking gives a person the energy to deal with difficult times. It toughens a person and makes them ready for anything. When you are mentally prepared to face anything, it is very easy to overcome anxiety and depression because you believe in your abilities as a person.

Someone might want to be positive-minded, but they do not know how to. The following tips will help someone struggling with negativity to turn the thoughts into positive thinking.

How to Be Positive Minded

- Identifying the situations that make you think negatively is essential. Is it that specific tasks at work make you feel some anxiety or depressed? Identify those things that make you have these feelings as the first remedy.

- Observe your thought patterns as frequently as possible. Knowing how you think will help you understand the times when you are most likely to have negative thoughts, and you can use that time to think positively.

- Allow yourself to be happy. Do not deny yourself the good things in life as this will make you anxious and depressed. Find out what makes you happy and go after it. Watch funny movies and laugh. Surround yourself with happy people and take every opportunity to be pleased as they are. Remember who you surround yourself with determines how you end up with. Two people struggling with anxiety and depression are most likely to damage each other.

- Strive to lead a healthy lifestyle because a healthy person is often positive minded. A healthy lifestyle includes regular exercise to help the mind relax and also exploring nature to find more things to be grateful for.

- Surround yourself with people. Being alone will only create room for you to be worried over things you have no control over. But being with people, mainly positive-minded people will distract you from any negative thinking that could lead to anxiety and depression. Avoiding people that are always negative is essential even as you try to interact. You would rather be by yourself than be surrounded by people who make you anxious and depressed or give more reasons over something you were trying to avoid.

- To be positive-minded, you have to practice for your mind to adapt to positivity. This includes talking to yourself regularly. It may sound funny at first to speak to yourself, but it is an excellent method. You know you better than anyone else. You understand how you would like to be motivated. Look at the mirror and talk to yourself. Tell yourself that everything is going to be alright and give yourself the positivity you need. You will find that by doing so and doing it frequently, you start being positive minded.

- Practice positive thinking with other people so that it becomes more and more a part of who you are. When you find someone struggling with negative thinking, talk to them, and encourage them as if you were encouraging yourself. This will also be helping you get rid of your anxiety and depression as you speak to the other person about their issue.

Positive thinking encourages a person to focus on positivity as a means of overcoming all the worries that could eventually lead to depression. This technique believes that the more you focus on negativity, the more likely you are to have anxiety and depression. This is true because negativity makes someone worried and stressed over things you have no control over. When you continue worrying, you eventually develop anxiety, and the fear leads to you having depression. Positive thinking, on the other hand, lets you go of things you are not in control of. Positive thinking gives you more reasons to be grateful for items that you may overlook. Sometimes things we have anxiety over are things that should not even be worrying us at all. It takes a positive minded person to see that letting go does us better than holding on to negativity.

Negativity discourages a person from taking risks because they think they did it before and failed and hence the anxiety to do it again. Positivity encourages letting go of the anxiety and depression and doing it all over again because every opportunity is a learning experience. Positivity will tell you to get rid of the anxiety and try again because this time you could do it and achieve.

Positive thinking encourages a person struggling with anxiety and depression to use a different strategy, while negativity will discourage somebody not to try because it seems too hard to tackle.

Positive thinking will tell someone to make use of everything they got in them to help the person overcome anxiety and depression while negativity will show a person that they are helpless, incapable, and not brave enough.

Positive thinking will help a person realize the mistake they made to get them into the situation while negative thinking will make someone think they got into anxiety and depression because they deserve it. Therefore, while a person who is thinking positively can try to fight with anxiety, a negative person will sink into self-sympathy and even give up on trying overcoming it.

Positive thinking will help someone see all the possibilities of working through anxiety and depression, while negative thinking will tell you it is useless trying to fight it because you will not achieve anything.

Positive thinking will encourage someone to talk to their family and friends or even professionals about their anxiety and depression. Negative thinking, on the other hand, will make a person think that no one can help and that it is in vain to talk it out. A person who is into positive thinking knows that there are people who believe in them while someone is into negative thinking thinks they are all alone and that no one cares enough to feel their pain.

Positive thinking is critical in all stages of anxiety and depression. In the early stages, a person will be able to let go of what is causing them anxiousness and depression. While in full-blown anxiety and depression, positive thinking will motivate a person to believe in their ability to overcome either by themselves or by getting help. After overcoming anxiety and depression, positive thinking encourages a person to continue with the technique so that they may not fall again back to where they came from.

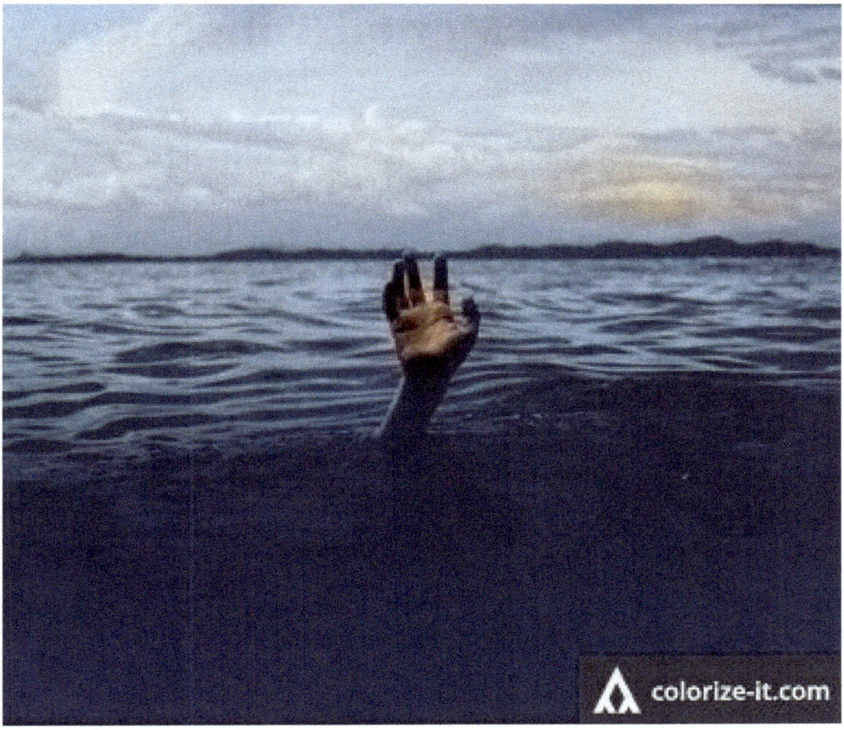
colorize-it.com

Chapter 10: Mental Toughness

In psychology, mental toughness is the strength and toughness in people that enables them to keep fighting through struggles until they succeed. Mental toughness can be natural or acquired over time. It is an important attribute to have in life as it enables you to cope better than your competitor with life's challenges and demands. Mental toughness can also make you resist changes in your life. How can we build mental toughness?

- Be emotionally stable to make excellent decisions even when under immense pressure.
- Be flexible and ready to adopt change.
- Believe in your abilities
- Be patient.
- Never compromise your standards.
- Be contented.
- Know that life gives you ups and downs.
- Stay positive even in negative situations.
- Never give up

Overcome Resistance That Keeps You from Moving Forward

We all have that voice in our head that discourages us from doing something. This voice tells you, "That is impossible" or "No, you can't do that. What will people think?" Sometimes the voice is our family and friends. That voice is resistance. What constitutes resistance?

- Overthinking
- Self-doubt
- Fear
- Time
- Little or no knowledge of how and where to start

So, how can we overcome this resistance and learn to move forward?

Who is in your inner circle?
Your inner circle constitutes of friends and family that you have opened your heart to. These people might either build you or break you. Your inner circle should constitute of few people that you can trust with your life. They should encourage you to achieve your goals and dreams in life. They should also be honest with you. In case of situations where they have a different opinion from you, they should stand their ground and at the same time show you love and support.

- **Become aware**
  Realizing and becoming aware that you are facing resistance enables you to fight and conquer it. I am in no way trying to say it is easy to become aware of resistance. No, it is the opposite. I mean, how can you become aware of something that you don't even think about; something that we don't even notice its presence? Our actions should help us achieve this milestone, but how? We should train ourselves to be aware of our actions. It will enable us to know when we are doing something that is not of importance at that specific time like a quick peek on our mail or a

distraction from the web instead of focusing on our work.

- **Define your daily tasks clearly and remain focused**
At every start of the day, make a list of tasks you intend to perform. You can define three important tasks and focus on them exclusively. After completing them, you can now concentrate on other smaller tasks. Defining your tasks prevents you from being lured into doing other things.

- **Get rid of distractions**
Many distractions are enticing, and if not checked, they can keep us away from moving forward. A distraction could be a friend, a family member, or the internet. Shut the internet for the whole of the time that you intend to work and inform your friends and family not to disturb you. Once that is done, start working and focus on your work only.

- **Set a time and place**
Set a start time of your day and stick to it always. Your most important work should be your priority in each day. It should be unique and different from each one of us but what is important is to have a specific start time and stick to it with no excuse.

- **Say 'No'**
Some people are naturally people's pleasers. Such people ignore their desires to uphold other people's desires. There is nothing wrong with saying 'No.'

Saying 'No' doesn't make you a selfish and mean person, but it helps you to focus on your life and follow your life course.

- **Just start**
  Now, all the above tips to overcome resistance are meaningless if you cannot start. The best way to overcome resistance is doing. It is not easy to start when you are feeling resistance but do start. Avoid distractions and keep reminding yourself why you need to start. Once you take that first step in starting, the work starts to flow.

What Are the Factors That Cause Mental Toughness?

Mental toughness is achieved through little objective wins. Sometimes mental toughness is about building our routine to enable us to conquer challenges through and through. People who are mentally tough need consistency. Different factors cause mental toughness. They are:

- **Fear of the unknown**
  Fear of the unknown, also known as xenophobia is the fear of going out of our comfort zone. It is an irrational feeling of fright about a place, person, or situation that we identify as new or strange. Fear of the unknown keeps us from indulging in new things or activities that would bring success or failure which we can learn from. This fear keeps us in our comfort zone. Let us look at what causes fear of the unknown in our lives.

- Negative past experiences like death or divorce.
- Insecurities
- Lack of self-confidence
- Poor knowledge about an issue.

Armed with the knowledge of what is fear of the unknown and what causes it, we can now look at how to overcome it.

- First, understand your fear
- The second is to find its root cause.
- Question it, keeping in mind that it is not based on reality.
- List and acknowledge failure as an option of the outcomes expected.
- Internalize with the fear and with time; it will subdue.
- Accept change and its effects.
- Train your mind to keep away from the fearful thoughts.

- **Lack of information**
Without proper information, most people would not dive into any opportunity. We would all want to know what we are indulging in even the risk-takers in life take risks with all information, including the results either the best possible outcome or worst possible outcome. Information is power, and lack of it makes us blind to where we are headed. It should not make you resist moving forward instead you should use all the available resources at your disposal to try and get as

much information as you can before you indulge in anything.

- **Fear of failure**
It is important to know that failure is part of life, and nobody enjoys it. Fear of failure keeps you from creativity and halts your progress. It causes self-doubt and can make you not uphold morality. What causes this failure? Let us look at the main reasons for its existence.

    - **Restrictive childhood** - Rules are good but just like everything else they can't extend to a certain limit. Some children were brought up with strict rules and ultimatum. These strict rules instilled fear in them and caused them always to seek reassurance and to always ask for consent before undertaking something. As adults, they bear this intense want for validation.
    - **Perfectionism** - the Perfectionist, fear to fail and are always terrified to get out of their comfort zone. They never want to try new things because they fear to fail. To them, failure is so awful that they never want to try. Perfectionists should learn that we win sometimes and sometimes we learn.

    - **Ego** - Ego makes some of us not to notice and appreciate the lessons that come with failure. Failure makes us want to try more and consequently brings us growth. Failure gives us life lessons on how not to give up but to keep striving.

- **Falsified self-confidence -** Self-confidence is important as it boosts our determination to do better in life. True self-confidence allows us to expect failure or success while on the other hand, the falsified one keeps us from achieving our true goals by avoiding risks. People with the latter self-confidence fear to indulge in new opportunities.

How can we overcome this fear of failure?

- **Find the root cause -** Try to get to the cause of your fear. Discovering and knowing the root cause of it reduces its power. Your fear could be by your insecurities or a big problem from your childhood. Whatever it is, find it out.

- **Readjust your goals** - Don't be rigid when planning out your goals. It is important to put in a certain allowance for failure and not expecting success all the time. As we said earlier, there are lessons to learn from failure. Failure does not make us weak, but through it, we become more enlightened.

- **Think positive** - We should realize that we are our thoughts, and as human beings, we tend to believe what we tell ourselves. Negative thoughts triggers fear in us. We should try and notice them and replace them with positive ones. The positive thoughts contribute greatly to our actions.

- **Envision all possible outcomes** - Uncertainties makes us scared, but when we know all the possible outcomes, we become prepared psychologically and get rid of uncertainties. Knowing how things could come out helps you to move forward.

- **Back up** - There is nothing that can give you a good kick to start than a backup plan. Remember a backup is not a plan to fail. It is an emergency door to take in case things don't go according to plan. A backup plan reduces our anxiety about failing.

- **Fear of disappointing others**
As human beings, we are wired to love and worry about other people, but when we start fearing to disappoint them, we will only be hurting ourselves. Fear of disappointing others is a negative emotion that keeps us away from our happiness. Let us learn some tips on how to triumph over this fear.

    - You should know that people's ideology on good behavior is never the same, and despite how much you try to please all of them, you will always disappoint some.
    - You should get out of your comfort zone to grow.

- Set up emotional boundaries and let your friends know that being kind is not being weak.
- Know that other people's reactions are not about you.
- Reassess your values and know what you would like for yourself

- **Fear of others' opinions**
What will people think? How will people view me? Have these questions ever stopped you from doing something? If yes, that is what fear of other people's opinions can cause. It makes you not to indulge in great things or otherwise. This fear stops you from achieving your true potential. We should learn to feel good and happy about our acts. It makes it easier to move forward without minding what other people will say about us.

- **Fear of not being able to do or learn something**
Some people resist new ideas or opportunities because they fear to be absolute. Every day we learn something new. Heck, we even learn new stuff from things we have been doing as a routine every day. If you don't learn directly from the idea, you will learn something from the people you will interact with along the way while implementing the idea. What are the fears that make up the fear of not being able to learn something?

    - **Fear of feeling stupid** - Do you fear to ask questions because by doing so, people might realize you are not as smart as you portray? If you fear to look stupid before others, speak lightly on the subject and inquire to know more. With that, the pressure reduces, and you can now learn anything you want from people.

- **Fear of more responsibilities** - Do you fear that if you learned new things that people will expect much from you? Such people fear to get out of routine until they give up on learning.

- **Not me** - Do you fear that you cannot learn as much as necessary from our education systems? With the way our learning institutions are structured, you might think that you cannot learn anything and that you are a failure when it comes to learning new things. It should not be the case as we can try different learning methods until we get one that will suit as and learn the concept.

Let us look at the way forward to overcome this fear.

- Shout out your fear
- Visualize yourself as capable.
- Do some physical exercises.
- Create a mantra
- Talk to someone about your fear.
- Unlearn your bad habit.

- **Laziness**

Laziness is an inclination that shows our lack of self-esteem. We all indeed get lazy sometimes, but no one wants to be. What causes laziness?

- Worry of producing substandard work.
- Confusion on what steps of a task to take first.
- Too much workload.
- Inability to ask for help.
- Fear of success and feelings of hopelessness.

How can we combat laziness?

- Allow yourself to fail, and guilt will eat you up.
- Learn to keep your word and follow through your commitments.
- Break your workload to small manageable tasks.
- Get a partner or a friend that will keep you responsible.

- **"Better a known evil than an unknown good."** When people avoid taking risks to do things, they are unsure of and instead follow the familiar steps they are sure of their outcomes, they are kept from moving forward. What people should know is that you can never know anything for certain as dynamics change every day. Opening up to new ideas and opportunities brings growth and life lessons.

Structural Resistances

In organizations, change brings growth, and we cannot escape from it due to political pressures, demographic characteristics, and technology. Resistance is a behavioral reaction by employees to real or imagined threats to their normalcy. What causes this resistance?

- **Fearing to fail** - Structural changes in an organization can make the employees doubt their potential. They acquire self-doubt, which makes them lose their self-confidence and inhibits their growth.
- **Loss of ranks** - Structural changes are met with resistance as they may try to change or get rid of some positions. People with some power and status will resist this change to protect their positions.
- **Breaking habits** - People love routine and will resist any change to a routine that the organizations may deem as unsuitable for current trends. They will resist structural changes to remain in their comfort zones. They are also aware of the time and energy needed to adapt to the new structural changes.
- **Conformity to group dynamics** - Group norms may not agree with the new structural changes. They may push employees to resist the changes.

Personal Resistance

Have you ever talked yourself out of moving forward with your plans and ambitions? Well, if yes then you've experienced resistance to moving forward. There are different ways that we talk ourselves out of our dreams and ambitions. They are:

- **Victim mentality**- We see ourselves as victims and at the mercy of everything and everyone around us. The victim always has reasons as to why they are not doing something. The only therapy for this is getting back your power, change your thoughts, and acts to be in line with your needs.

- **Route plan B-** You make plans and set goals, but once you learn of the requirements needed to achieve the goals, your initial excitement wears off, and you start looking for plan B route. Train yourself to have confidence and to stick to one goal at a time. Seeing your goals through to success opens doors for growth. Be your own cheerleader and find people that will encourage you to persist.

- **I hate change-** Personal change helps you grow and achieve your dreams. You keep telling yourself that routine is good as with it there is a certainty. Keep reminding yourself that everything is subject to change.

- **I am ever stressed-** You do things in a hurry and never enjoy your life journey. In your plans, there is always something you need to do before you rest and relax. It is not healthy, and it is good to learn to achieve things happily.

- **Mask wearer-** You never reveal your true self to people. You keep acting okay even when you are having problems in achieving your goals. Love yourself and know your value. Don't be bothered by other people's opinions.

After understanding how you have been resisting moving forward, a new you are born. You become a strong and determined person who keeps moving forward even after experiencing challenges. How can you overcome personal resistance to moving forward?

- Discover your ideal method for resisting growth out of past experiences.
- Find role models to look up to.
- Develop pep talks to encourage you to move forward.

CPSIA information can be obtained
at www.ICGtesting.com
Printed in the USA
BVHW052024060921
616156BV00002B/112

9 783986 530266